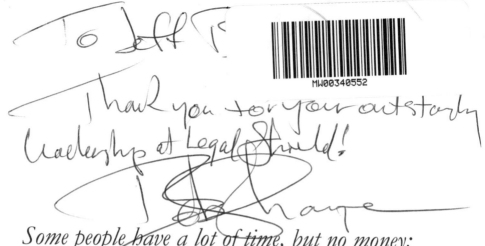

Some people have a lot of time, but no money;
It's because they don't work hard enough.
Some people have a lot of money but no time;
It's because they don't work smart enough.
The most successful people have both.

You can't go back and change the past,
But you can start now and change the future.
What's holding you back?

How to Be a Network Marketing Millionaire

Bob Sharpe, CAS
www.ITrainMillionaires.com

How to Be a Network Marketing Millionaire

Published by Bob Sharpe

Copyright © 2011 Bob Sharpe

Printed in the United States of America

The author does not, in any way, make any warranty, guarantee or representation expressed or implied, as to the income, profits or success of the individual distributor who reads this book. Actual success varies based upon many factors, including the teachability, work ethic, natural skills and abilities and number of contacts made by the individual distributor. It also depends on the stability, products, pricing structure and compensation plan of the network marketing company.

Nothing herein should be taken as legal or tax advice.

ISBN: 978-0615556543

Dedication

This book is dedicated to
My Mom and Dad
Who taught me that
Profit is better than a salary
And
A Business is better than a job.

It is also dedicated to
The many people in my upline
Who made my success possible,
And
The wonderful people in my downline
Who helped make it happen
In the amazing
Network marketing industry.

Table of Contents

Table of Contents

1 Network Marketing as a Profession

About 15 years ago I was taking a business course in a major university when one of the students asked the professor about network marketing. "I don't recommend it," he responded. Then he began to list his reasons.

A few years later same professor gave up his post at the university. Today, 15 years later, the wise professor is a successful network marketer himself.

I am a professional network marketer. I chose network marketing as a career and diligently applied myself to it, just as a doctor would apply himself to the field of medicine. Within a few years, I began earning more money than many professionals in other fields, and my income was residual income.

Most people start their network marketing careers part time while they are working a regular job.

- You don't need to go to school to become a professional network marketer. You can get excellent on-the-job training.
- You start earning money right away instead of waiting until you get out of your training program.
- Top earning network marketers are some of the highest paid professionals in the world. How many careers do you know

in which people can earn $100,000 to $1,000,000 or more per month in lifetime residual income?

- Network marketers can earn lifetime residual income.
- Network marketers don't have to worry about being laid off
- Network marketing allows people to have control of their lives. They can work when they want, vacation when they want, sleep as late as they want . . . and they never have to miss their kids' soccer games because of work.
- Network marketers in the US get better legal tax breaks than almost anybody.

There are so many advantages to network marketing; it's a wonder that most network marketers don't take their businesses very seriously.

You can become outrageously successful in your network marketing career. You can change your life. Just learn and practice the things that bring success. Do it regularly for a few years and your life can change dramatically.

Follow the Golden Path to Fortune

Regardless of the hype you may have heard, network marketing is not a magic wand. There is no such thing as a magic zap that will fill your downline with people and your mailbox with checks. If that's what you're looking for, try Vegas or the Lottery. You might get lucky and become that 1 in a gazillion to become the next gambling millionaire.

Network marketing is the golden path that starts where you are and ends in the income stratosphere. You don't know it, but some of the wealthiest people in your city are network marketers. You won't find them in the business section of your local paper or on the evening news. You will find them at the country club that you can't afford to join, and lounging around the world's premiere resorts. You will also find them at their companies' national conventions and top producer trips.

The Golden Path of network marketing leads to the massive passive income that can give you the time and money to do the things you've always wanted to do.

Got that? You can have the time and money to be able to do the things you always wanted to do. What would it be worth to you to live the rest of your life like that? What would you be willing to do to have it? It is possible, and you can have it. The Golden Path will get you there.

It doesn't come randomly to a few. It doesn't come by chance or luck. It comes by discovering the Golden Path, by learning the simple skills, and by following the Path to its destination. Just like an Interstate freeway, if you travel the Path far enough, you will arrive at the destination.

Yes, you have to invest a small amount of time and money to enter and follow the Golden Path. If you learn the skills and follow the path, the rewards you'll get are mind boggling.

The people who didn't follow the Path will tell you it can't be done. The people who did can show you that it happens to everyone who follows the Path far enough.

The Path is not always easy. It will lead you through the valleys of despair as well as the peaks of elation. You'll pass a countless number of exits and U-turn lanes along the way, but you must keep traveling the Path if you want to have all the time and money to be able to have the lifestyle of your dreams.

You'll pass through deserts and ascend some steep inclines. When you enter the Promised Land, you'll find it's the Land of Time and Money – YOUR time and YOUR money!

The Golden Path is waiting for you. What will you do?

Your future is in your hands. Come and join us at the top.

Ask Your Boss

What do you think would happen if you walked into your boss's office tomorrow and said:

Boss, I'd like to renegotiate my compensation with this company. This is how I want to get paid:

1. Do you remember the work I did for you the first month I was with the company? I'd like to get paid for it again. In fact, I'd like to get paid for it over and over again every month.

2. Then I'd like to get paid for the work I did the second month – over and over again every month. I'd like that for the third and fourth months and every month I work for you so that I'm getting paid every month over and over again for all the work I ever did for you.

3. When I refer a new employee to the company and you hire them, I'd like to get paid for their work too, and I'd like to get paid the same way you will be paying me. You know, I want to get paid over and over again every month for all the work they do.

4. When referrals refer an employee and you hire him, I'd like to get paid for his work, over and over. I'd like you to pay me for the new employees they refer too, down to the 6th or 7th level.

5. One more thing. I want you to pay me when I'm not working, like when I want to take a 3-month vacation or I just don't feel like coming to work.

OK?

My Story Can Become Your Story

Very few people in network marketing take it as seriously as a career. They have their careers, which they take very seriously. Then they try a networking opportunity "to see if it works out." They'll:

- Spend a few dollars to join a company
- Spend a few hours to try it
- Talk to a few people about the business
- Then they'll quit, saying, "Network marketing just didn't work for me."

If an aspiring accountant approached accounting that way, or if an aspiring Realtor® approached real estate that way, they would, of course, fail miserably. Why should network marketing be any different?

I was involved in several network marketing opportunities before I became successful in the business. I approached them that way – hoping they would work out, hoping people would magically appear in my downline and do a lot of business so I could get make a lot of money for doing next to nothing. It was the Lottery Mentality. You know – you spend a little money and hope to strike it rich.

Then I was in a company where I made about $20,000 over a 3-year span. I learned some of the skills, and when I put them into practice, it began to work. Our product was hard for me to sell, however, because very few people thought they needed it, so I was always trying to jump hurdles to make sales.

While I was doing that, I was invited to join a company where sales were much easier, overrides were much higher, and I joined. In a short time I became one of the top leaders in California, and we began to enjoy the lifestyle we had always dreamed about. I tried to get my wife to quit her job, but she wouldn't quit. I then got her fired (not on purpose) by taking her on too many vacations! When she needed a new car, I bought her a new Camry with the extra money I got from one month's pay increase. It was probably the biggest pay increase I ever made in a month, and it bought her a new car.

Why did I suddenly succeed after all the years of failure and mediocrity I had experienced in network marketing? I can think of a few reasons:

"I have failed over and over and over. That's why I succeeded."
--Michael Jordan

1. **I had learned from my failures.**

   I had become thoroughly versed in *what not to do*. It convinced me to look at the other side of the success coin and thoroughly learn *what to do to be successful.*

2. **I had begun to learn recruiting and team-building.**

   I was also fortunate to have two people in my downline who were very good team builders. My success came more from them than from me at first, because I was still learning how to follow *The Way of Success.*

3. **I was on a team with very good upline support.**

My team leader provided a training web site, training conference calls, recruiting conference calls, a sizzle line and replicated websites for his team members. He also served as my upline mentor, since he was the one who had recruited me.

4. **I had made some very good contacts from my previous experiences.**

I invited them to join my next business. Several of them did, and some of them became stars. I was blessed to have several team members become successful in the business during my first year. No, I didn't become filthy rich, but over the next few years I made half a million dollars working part time. Half of the months I spent in the business I hardly worked at all. That is the power of residual income.

5. **For the first time, I began treating my network marketing activities as a career and as a real business.**

I devoured the training, got passionate about the business, generated lots of leads and built a training web site with lots of tools and trainings for my team. My team members brought on a lot of people who became successful in the business. Within a few years I had 3 team members making over $100,000 per year and quite a few others making a full-time income, and most of them did this by working the business part-time.

The nice thing about network marketing is that when your downline team makes money, you make money. When your team makes a lot of money, you make a lot of money. It doesn't happen by accident or by luck. It happens by learning some simple skills, going to work with them and sharing them with your downline. You'll find that theme over and over in this book because it is so crucial to success, and so neglected by most network marketers.

You don't have to be a rocket scientist or a PhD to learn the skills. You don't even have to be a high school graduate. Just master the skills and go to work.

Network marketing is the best opportunity for ordinary people to make extraordinary incomes and change their lives. I have seen doctors and lawyers do so well in network marketing that they closed their practices. I have also seen school bus drivers and janitors with little education become 6-figure earners.

All it takes is a great desire for something better and an unswerving commitment to make it happen.

It can happen to you too, if you make it happen. Network marketing gives economic power to the people more than any other career option. That power is available to you.

What will you do with it?

2 Will Network Marketing Work for You?

Many people enter network marketing with a desire for something better, but without a strong determination to make it happen. They say, "I'll give it a try." No. You don't give it a try. You get in there and do it, or it won't work.

It's no different from anything else in life. If you give marriage "a try," you'll be divorced in 2 years. If you give your job "a try," you'll be out the door in months. If you give school "a try," you'll end up dropping out or flunking out.

Network Marketing Is Like Baking a Cake

If you have a good recipe for baking a cake, and if you follow the recipe *exactly,* do you have any doubt as to how the cake will turn out? No. It will turn out exactly as planned. If you bake 1,000 cakes with the same recipe, and you follow the recipe exactly each time, you will get a perfect cake each time, assuming you have a good recipe.

You know what you are going to do. You know what you are going to get.

Network marketing isn't quite as exact as baking a cake. For instance, you might follow a great system exactly, and you might end up making $20,000 a month. Another person might also follow the same system exactly and might end up making $70,000 a month. Why is that? It's because unlike flour, sugar and eggs, people are all different. Your friend might work harder than you. She might have better skills or better connections. Also, your friend might recruit a superstar who is worth $30,000 a month to her, and you might build your organization without the blessing of having a superstar for a while.

However, if you learn some simple skills and follow the principles of success, you will be successful. Some people will make it faster than others. Some will go higher than others. But success is available to all who follow the path and pay the price.

It's very predictable. If you do what is required for success in network marketing, you will become very successful in time. For most successful network marketers, it's 1 to 5 years.

Network Marketing Is the Easiest Way to Make a Big Income

Let's say you want to become a dentist. You will have 4 years of undergraduate study. The cost? 4 years of your time, a lot of hard work and $100,000 or more for school. Then you will have 4 more years of dental school at a cost of $150,000 to $250,000. You will have spent 8 years, thousands of hours and at least $250,000 before you are even qualified to earn money in your chosen profession.

Then, if you start your own practice, it will cost you $150,000 or more just to open your practice. How much will you make? According to Salary.com, that the 2011 U.S. national average

Here's how it can look:

	You	The Dentist
Cost of training	$0	$300,000 or more
Years of training	0	8
Hours per week in work or study	40	40
Cost of starting business	$100-$500	$150,000 or more
First 4 year earning potential	$25,000-$100,000 or more	$0 – still in school
Annual income after 8 years	$50,000 to $1,000,000	$0 – just graduated
Residual income potential	Unlimited	None

In short, by the time the future dentist graduates and is ready to start his career, you can be retired on $100,000 to over $1,000,000 per year.

If you are as diligent at learning the skills and working the business as a dentist or other successful professional, there is no reason you cannot succeed big in network marketing. You can do it in much less time and at much lower cost than other professionals in their careers.

The problem is, as easy as it is to learn to be successful, and as easy as it is to follow the path of success, it's even easier to not do it. When it comes to success in network marketing, most people take the easiest path – the path of doing the bare minimum, or even nothing at all. That's the path to failure.

Most aspiring network marketers fail because they don't do what it takes to be successful.

| See no Prospects | Hear no Training | Speak no Business | Make no Money |

How to Be Successful in Any Career – Including Network Marketing

The game is scheduled, and we have to play it.
We might as well win it.
--Sign in Boston Celtics locker room

The formula is not difficult. The skills are probably simpler than the skills you are using on your job now. Just master them, go to work with them every day, and you have no limitations on your future income.

1. Learn the skills
2. Practice and perfect the skills
3. Go to work every day
4. Follow the directions for success
5. Don't quit
6. Continue going to work every day.

Simple, isn't it? If you don't do these things at your job, you'll get fired. If you don't do them in your network marketing business, you'll fail.

It's the same thing...

Do what it takes to be successful, and you'll succeed.
Don't do what it takes to be successful, and you'll fail.

In any organization of any size, there are a lot of people at the bottom and only a few at the top. There is a reason that some rose to the top and others didn't. If you ask 100 of the "top people" how they got there, you'll hear 100 versions of the same story.

I asked the manager of my credit union how he got to be manager. He said, "I started as a teller 11 years ago. I was always willing to do the extra things that many of the other employees wouldn't do, and I got promoted."

The same is true in network marketing. The people who learn the skills and use them every day can make a lot more money in network marketing than they can on their jobs. The people who do the extras own the key to the vault.

The Story of 2 Brothers

The person who gets the farthest is generally the one who is willing to do and dare.
The sure-thing boat never gets far from shore.
–Dale Carnegie

Rob and Sam graduated from college together and embarked on their careers. They both went into the same industry – cell phones. Their career paths, however, were vastly different from each other's.

Sam's Cell Phone Store

Sam took a position as a management trainee in a cell phone store. He got excellent training in product knowledge and in-store sales. He started out with a small salary and small commissions on the phones he sold. His small commissions were made up, in part, by the fact that the store had a lot of walk-in customers, so he sold a lot of phones.

Several months later, when he was promoted to Assistant Manager, his pay went up, and he started working 50-55 hours a week. Two years later, when he was given his own store to manage, he had the privilege of working 55-60 hours a week. He was making $65,000 a year.

He saved up his money to open his own cell phone store. A few years later, he had $35,000 in savings. He borrowed $65,000 from his brother Rob, who was making a lot of money by that time. That's how he got the $100,000 to invest in his store.

The first few months he was working 75 hours a week and not making any money, but he had his own store, and he knew that he would start making money after the first year in business.

After a few years in the store, he finally started making $100,000 a year, and he was able to cut his working hours back to 40-50 hours a week.

Rob's Network Marketing Cell Phone Business

While finishing up his last semester of college, a friend told Rob about a network marketing opportunity with cell phones and other telecommunication services. Rob wanted to join, but he decided to put it off a few months until after his final exams.

The week after graduation, Rob got a job. Then he invested $500 to start his network marketing business. His sponsor taught him the simple skills his second day in the business. He was new on a full-time job, so he only had 7-10 hours a week to devote to his new business.

Rob tried to recruit his brother Sam into the business. Sam said he was more comfortable working a "real" job in the cell phone store. He knew he would be promoted to manager in a matter of time.

Rob's sponsor told him about the taxes he could save by having a qualifying home business. Rob got the book from Resources section of www.ITrainMillionaires.com and learned that his home business gave him extra tax deductions that would save him $4,000 in income taxes. He followed the instructions from the book and filled out a new W4 form with his employer. That month he took home $320 more in his paycheck because his employer did not have to withhold as much tax money. He used the extra money to go to his company's conventions so he could learn more and get more motivation to build his business.

Working with his sponsor, who served as his upline mentor, Rob quickly got 5 customers and 3 people to join his downline. He earned a $300 bonus his first month and earned back his entire startup investment. His second month he earned a $300 bonus. 7 months later, Rob quit his job and went full-time in his network marketing business.

Rob was thankful that he had a successful sponsor and who served as his upline mentor to help him and lead him to success in the business.

By the end of his first year, Rob was earning $5,000 a month in residual income. He worked very hard and followed all the principles of network marketing success. At that time his brother Sam was earning $3,500 a month as the assistant manager of the cell phone store.

Two years later, Rob was making $32,000 a month in residual income, and he could take time off any time he wanted (he took 4 vacations that year). Sam was working 55-60 hours a week – every week – for a little over $5,000 a month. "At least I've got benefits," Sam thought to himself.

Many successful network marketers have had traditional businesses in the past. I recently met a man who had owned a number of Nextel cell phone stores in Philadelphia. When Nextel was bought out by Sprint, he suddenly began losing money. He joined a network marketing business. After a few years he was earning more money than he ever dreamed he could make by owning the stores. His income soared without leases, employees, workers comp, customer service or any of the other hassles of owning a traditional business. Was he happy he discovered network marketing? You bet!

The chart below shows the difference between the income and lifestyle potentials of a traditional businesses and a network marketing business in the illustration of Sam and Rob.

Sam and Rob's Phone Business Careers Compared

	Sam	Rob
Career	Cell Phone Store	Network Marketing
Initial Investment	$100.000	$500
Borrowed to start business	$65,000	None
Monthly Fixed Expenses	$11,450	$30
Hours worked per week	50-60	20-25
First Year Income (Loss)	($45,000)	$5,500
Fourth Year Income	$80,000	$196,000
Debt after 4 Years	$44,000	NONE
8th Year Income	$120,000	$776,000
8th Year Hours Work per Week	50-60	10-20
Vacation days per year	10	200

3 Advantages of a Network Marketing Career

Network marketing is an excellent career choice for many reasons. Here are some of them:

1. It's Easy to Get in.

You don't have to send out resumes and drag yourself to countless job interviews and compete with hundreds of candidates.

Network marketing business-people are always looking for good candidates, and they always have room for more.

2. You Are in Control of Your Job Search

Every network marketing businessperson will want to bring you on. If you look at several opportunities, you can choose any one of them to join. You are in complete control of the "hiring" process.

It is important to make a wise decision here. You want to select a good company that markets products or services that are in demand. You also want to select your upline sponsor carefully. We'll give you information to help you decide later in the book.

3. The Investment Is Small to have Your own Business.

- Where else can you start a business for $500 or less?
- How many businesses can you start by charging a credit card?
- How many businesses can you start and recover your entire investment in a month or two?

In addition, the tax savings you receive with a qualifying home business are often greater than the entire cost of starting and running your network marketing business. That means that, even if you have difficulty making money at first, you will still come out ahead financially, unless you are in a company that requires you to buy a lot of products on an expensive monthly purchase on autoship.

4. The Overhead Is Low

Since you are running your business from your home, there is no additional rent to pay. You have no employees, no insurance, other expenses are minimal, and they're all tax deductible.

5. The Risk Is Very Low.

Even if you fail, and even if you don't take the tax advantages available to you, the most you can lose is a few hundred bucks. And that's a worst case scenario.

Last month a business consultant spoke in our local Chamber of Commerce breakfast meeting. He told the story of a couple he knew who invested $200,000 to start a restaurant. They lost it all in a year. You couldn't lose $200,000 in network marketing, even if you tried hard to do it. It happens regularly in traditional businesses.

6. It's Easy to Learn.

You can learn the basic skills in a few hours and perfect them in a few months as you work your business. Most training is free. Some training costs a little, and you can earn while you are learning.

7. You Can Work Anywhere.

Have you always wanted to live by the beach or in the mountains? You can move almost anywhere and still be successful in your business. With the Internet and unlimited long distance phone services, it's easier now than ever before. You can even spend summers in Minnesota and winters in Florida if you want. You're in control, and it really feels good.

8. You Can Set Your Own Hours.

Take time off every week for your daughter's soccer game, your son's trumpet lessons and Bible study at your church. You don't have to get permission from your boss, because you're the boss!

9. You Get Residual Income.

In the right kind of company, every time you get a customer, you get paid over and over again. You also get paid residual income on the work done by your downline.

It's an exhilarating feeling to know that $1,000's will come in every month whether you work or not. That's the power of residual income.

Retirement is not an age. It's an income level.
--Brian Tracy

4 Network Marketing Is Not What it Used to Be

Rrrrring Rrrrring Rrrrring

"Hello."

"Hey Bob!" the excited voice on the other end belted out. "I've found this company that has a fantastic plan for us to join and get rich! They're having a meeting tonight, and I want you to come and join me."

I went to the meeting, not knowing what to expect. I sat there for an hour watching a persuasive presenter draw circles on a board. He explained how easy it is for anyone to join the company and get rich.

"All you have to do is recruit 10 people," he explained. "Then they each recruit 10. Then they each recruit 10 more people. Then in that group each recruits 10 and they in turn recruit 10 more people apiece. That's all you have to do to become a millionaire. It's so easy anyone can do it."

My head was spinning from all the circles. At the end of the meeting, a group of people circled around me like buzzards circling their prey. "Join us and get rich," one man said.

"How much are you making?" I queried.

"I'm not making anything yet," he replied, "but I'm gonna be rich."

Network marketing has changed since those early days. Thank God it has changed.

From the Hyped Up Meetings to the Professional

High-pressure, circles-on-the-board meetings still occur, but most successful career network marketers don't do the buzzard thing. Today it's more businesslike. That's why network marketing is attracting educated successful people. When they see the power of the opportunity, many of them become interested.

Many of today's network marketing presentations are operated on a professional level, educating prospects about the possibilities and motivating – rather than pressuring – them to take the next step.

Professional presentations create an entirely different atmosphere. It's not the get-rich-quick pitch for some of the lower and lower-middle class people who want a quick way up in life. It's the presentation of a highly profitable business model for professional people who are open to creating new profit centers or who just want to get their lives back.

B2B Network Marketing

B2B stands for Business to Business, while B2C stands for Business to Consumer. Most businesses specialize in either one focus or the other. Some businesses, such as Office Depot and Costco cater to both.

When network marketing companies developed competitively-priced products and services that were useful for businesses, it opened an entirely new marketplace – and respectability – for network marketing. A B2B network marketer can fit right into professional business associations and chamber of commerce meetings with an image just as professional as local traditional brick and mortar businesspeople.

In that context, you want to go in overtly as a sales rep and covertly as a recruiter. While you are publicly seeking clients, you are also looking for good prospects to recruit into your business.

In the early days of network marketing, almost all the products sold were high-priced vitamins and soaps. True, they were probably better quality than similar products in the stores, but they were often double, triple or even quadruple the prices. Were they really 2-4 times better to justify the prices? And why would I want to pay 200% more for a product that was only 20% better?

Today, many types of products and services are available through network marketing, and many of them with very competitive pricing.

Respectable Companies Use Network Marketing

Sprint used network marketing years ago to build a large customer base quickly. Mary Kay is one of the most respected names in cosmetics, and Avon turned to network marketing to build their business a few years ago.

Network Marketing Is Taught in a Major University

Dr. Charles King, of the University of Illinois has been teaching a class on network marking since the 1990's. As a Harvard graduate, he has been invited to the Harvard Business School to speak on network marketing.

Also, the University of Texas El Paso (UTEP) College of Business Administration has sponsored various events exploring the value of network marketing. Other colleges, including Utah Valley State College and California Lutheran University are beginning to see the value of network marketing.1.

Bethany College in Kansas recently started a degree program in network marketing. The announcement was made on their web site on April 5, 2011. See the Appendix for the article.

Wealth Experts Endorse Network Marketing

Donald Trump has not only endorsed network marketing, but in March, 2011, he spent 2 hours on his hit TV show, The Celebrity Apprentice, featuring a network marketing company and one of their products.

Other wealth experts who wholeheartedly recommend network marketing are Robert Allen, Brian Tracy, Robert Kiyosaki, author of Rich Dad Poor Dad, and the late Jim Rohn. At least 2 of the above-named people are actively involved in network marketing themselves.

---

[1] Michael L. Sheffield, The Academy of Network Marketing?, www.sheffieldnet.com/srn_artice6.html

Network Marketing Is Not What it Used to Be

Of course there are always the scams and bad practitioners who give networking a black eye, but that is true of every industry. In evaluating an industry, it is important to look at the legitimate practitioners, not just the crooks and scams.

The Internet and inexpensive unlimited long distance make network marketing easier and more profitable than ever before.

Many network marketing companies offer web sites and online videos for their distributors. Using the Internet and the phone, many network marketers are able to do most of their work in their pajamas. And many of them do.

5 Why Some Network Marketers Fail and Others Succeed

The rules for successful careers are the same for network marketers and employees. Many people who are successful employees are failures at network marketing. The overwhelmingly common reason is that they don't follow the same rules for their network marketing careers as they do for their jobs. In a nutshell, these rules are:

1. Learn the necessary skills
2. Schedule your work time (in most jobs, your company will do that for you).
3. Go to work on time every day.
4. Do your work diligently.
5. Don't leave work early.
6. Keep learning new job skills as necessary
7. Don't quit

You have to do those things to keep your job. Are you willing to do them for your network marketing business?

Almost everybody who has a successful network marketing career follows these rules religiously.

If you are not willing to do what successful network marketers do, you are guaranteed to fail. Don't get involved in network marketing.

Believe in Yourself

"If you think you can do it,
or you think you can't do it, you are right."
--Henry Ford

Can you succeed? Of course you can! But you have to follow the directions! Do you believe you can succeed? Look at it this way:

> **If others can have successful**
> **network marketing careers**
> **you can too.**

Why not? Are all the successful people better at it than you? Of course they are. Were they always better than you? Absolutely not! They learned and practiced their skills.

The reason the successful people are where they are is that they learned the skills and made the sacrifices needed to get to where they are. You can do it too. You just have to do it the way they did.

If there is one message I want you to get out of this book, it's this:

> **You can become fabulously successful**
> **in network marketing**
> **IF you learn the skills, follow the directions,**
> **go to work and give it time to build.**

The 2-Step to Network Marketing Success

1. Know (learn) what it takes to be successful.
2. Do it.

Those who take action get success; those who don't get whatever is left.

Plan to Succeed

Dr. Elmer Towns, of Liberty University, wrote a lot of books on why some churches grow, inter-viewed a young pastor who had planted a new church. The church had grown to a membership of over 1,000 in a few years.

He asked the young pastor, "Were you surprised to see how much your church grew?"

"No," answered the pastor. "I expected it to grow large. When I came to this city to start the church, it was already large in my mind and large in my heart."

The young pastor had a big plan. He did the things necessary to accomplish it, and to get the blessing of God on his work.

Plan to succeed. Have a goal. Go for the goal and never slow down or turn away from it until you get there.

The Road Map to Success

Success is a journey. You have a starting point, and you have a destination. As long as you continue traveling toward your destination, you'll make it.

If you stop or get sidetracked and turn off the highway, you'll never reach your destination of success.

If you slow down too much, you might get there too late.

If you stay on the right road and continue making reasonable progress, you'll eventually arrive at the destination.

I've driven from the Los Angeles area to Detroit so many times I could probably do it with my eyes closed (I'm not going to try).

Every time I make the trip, the same thing happens. I drive a couple hours, and I always stop at the same spot in Barstow, California, to take a break. I look at the odometer and calculate that I've only gone 3-4% of the journey. And, without fail, the thought pops into my head, "It's so far. It will take forever to get there."

Then, when I turn in for the night, I look at the map in my hotel room and see that I've made significant progress that day. A couple days later I'm there.

Keep moving on the road to success. Always move in the right direction. Don't get sidetracked and turn down another road. You'll get there.

Life often throws you a curve. Unexpected things happen. Sometimes bad things happen. They happen to everybody. Successful people learn how to handle them, pick themselves up and continue on the path to success. Take care of the bad things, pick yourself up and keep on going.

You've got to Move On

On one of the trips – from Detroit to L.A. – we had an accident and totaled our car on the Texas-New Mexico State line – a very remote area of the country. It was a two-State accident. I feel asleep at the wheel and hit a sign in Texas. When the car stopped rolling, we were in New Mexico. It was a two-time-zone accident. It started at 10:30 PM Central Time and ended at 9:30 PM Mountain Time!

A deputy sheriff picked us up and drove us to a motel for the night. In the morning we contacted a wrecker who took the car off the highway. We signed what was left of the car over to him. Then we took a bus from San Jon, New Mexico to Albuquerque, and then a flight to L.A. Although we had had a major setback, we picked ourselves up and continued on our journey. Had we not moved on, we would still be in San Jon, New Mexico today – over 30 years later!

Even though we suffered a major loss, we stuck to our goal, quickly initiated a workable Plan B and continued on to our destination. If you encounter a major obstacle (and you will), get up and get moving as quickly as you can. And make sure you continue to move in the right direction.

What is holding you back? Do you want to stay where you are? You will, unless you do something about it. Bad stuff happens to all of us. Everybody who knows me agrees that I've gone through more than my share, but I don't want to bore you with my story. I had to learn to overcome the setbacks. You do, too.

What do you want your life to be like 5 years from now? The good news is that you can make the decisions that will change your life. And outside of getting a big inheritance from a rich uncle (it ain't gonna happen), network marketing is the best way for an ordinary individual to develop an affluent lifestyle within a few short years.

People from all walks of life and all education levels have found financial freedom in network marketing. It all revolves around finding the right skills, using them every day and instilling them into your downline.

We Have Met the Enemy and It Is Us

. . . so said Pogo in an old newspaper comic strip. You can be your worst enemy in your network marketing business if you're not careful.

The activities of success are easy to do. They are even easier not to do. You have to decide that you will do them. And you have to stick to your plan, no matter what.

Don't sabotage your success and your future. You will live the rest of your life in the future, so make it a good one.

Why Some Fail and Others Succeed

Here are some of the ways network marketers mess up their success and their future:

The Comfort Zone

> *Life begins at the end of your comfort zone.*
> —Neale Donald Walsch

You have to get out of your comfort zone to be successful in business. How many other times in life do you have to get out of your comfort zone?

When the alarm rings at 6:00 AM Monday morning, does that wake you out of your comfort zone? What about being stuck in traffic on the way to work? Or missing your kid's soccer game because you had to work?

Procrastination

You think you can always do it later, but can you really? Theoretically, you can, but you won't. Why won't you? Because you're in the habit of procrastinating. If you were not in the habit, you wouldn't have been thinking of doing it later. You would have already started on it.

Do you really want the lifestyle of your dreams? Is it worth working for – especially if you can accomplish it in a few years? Yes, it IS worth working for. Do you want it sooner, or do you want it later? The sooner you get going, the sooner you'll have it.

Discouragement

The devil was having a garage sale. He was selling his tools. Some of his tools were selling for $50; others for $100. One tool, however, had a $5 Million price tag on it.

"Why is that tool so expensive?" a visitor asked.

"Oh, that's my best tool," replied the devil. "I can destroy more network marketers with that tool than any other tool."

That tool was DISCOURAGEMENT.

What discourages you?

Maybe it's when you have your heart set on recruiting the person who would be perfect for your business. You know, the person who is going to build a big downline and make you a millionaire. Then the person decides not to join – or joins another networking business.

Maybe it's when everybody seems to be saying "no," or when your best friend says something bad about your company. Or maybe it's when you can't get anyone in your downline to take the business seriously.

We all get discouraged at times. It's natural. It's only human. The thing that separates the winners from the losers is what they do when they get discouraged.

What do YOU do when you get discouraged?

Realize that it's not the end of the world. Other people are successful in network marketing. There is no reason why you can't succeed too, unless you fail to do the things it takes to be a success.

Take a breather. Read – or listen to – a good book on success. Call your upline mentor. Then determine to go on.

Check the Resource Page at www.ITrainMillionaires.com for the good stuff the read and listen to.

Remember, we didn't win all the battles in World War II. In fact, we lost a lot of them, but we did win the war. You will lose some battles along the way. Everybody does. But you can win the war. You must win the war. Life is too precious to miss the lifestyle of your dreams. It's too short to put it off. Nobody said it would be easy. But it's a lot easier than living your whole life and missing it.

It is a tragic thing to miss out on the lifestyle you could have had. Don't let discouragement stop you from having it. It's a lot closer than you think when you're on track and progressing toward it.

A few years ago I read that the average American watches TV 6 hours a day. That's 42 hours a week. Most people would more than double their incomes if they spent some of that 42 hours learning and working instead of watching TV. Would doubling your income change your life and your future?

No, I'm not suggesting working an extra 42 hours a week. But what do you think would happen if you cut back on the TV and spent 1-2 hours a day doing something constructive to improve your life?

Turn the TV off and spend the time working on your business. If you've run out of people to talk to, buy some leads and call them (we'll discuss buying leads later in this book). Or go somewhere where there are people you can talk to. Prospects for your business are everywhere. You can find them if you'll go looking for them. And you'll catch a lot of them if you use the right bait and use it skillfully.

Fear of Rejection

Do you feel bad when people say "no?" Just realize that most people are going to say no. It will always be that way.

Some people are fearful of starting a business. It's not your fault.

Some people don't have the money to start. It's not your fault.

Some people may have failed in the past, and they don't want to try again. It's not your fault.

Some people think they're just too busy to change their lives. It's not your fault.

Some people might not like network marketing. It's not your fault.

Some people are so negative they just say no to everything. It's not your fault.

Get it? When people say no, it's not your fault, unless you give an absolutely lousy presentation. If you talk to enough people, you'll even recruit some with a lousy presentation. As you give more presentations, you will get better. And you will recruit more people. They are not rejecting you!

Perfectionism

Several years ago, a very nice lady joined our business. She brought her husband to the interview. He was very supportive of her desire to build a business.

She became a student of the service we sold. She showed me her notebook. I had never seen anyone who had put together such a well organized, comprehensive book of materials for building the business.

"I want to make sure I do everything right," she told me.

I encouraged her to make her list and to let me help her contact her prospects. Every time I called her, she told me she wasn't ready yet, because she still didn't have everything just right.

After a few months she quit, without ever recruiting anyone or selling one thing.

In all the history of the world, only one perfect being ever walked this earth, and that's not us.

You won't be perfect, so don't worry about it. Just learn how to make a presentation and practice it. Get your upline mentor to help you talk to your people when you get started and move ahead. You'll never be perfect, but you'll get closer to it as you make more and more presentations.

Listening to the Wrong People

When you start your network marketing business, it's amazing how many people will tell you how impossible it is to make money in network marketing. Some of them tried and failed. Others have friends who tried and failed. They might be

well-meaning friends, but wouldn't it be better to listen to successful people than to the people who failed and quit? After all, the experts are the people who are the people who are successful, not the people who failed and quit, or the people who got involved.

Listen to the people who are successful in the business. They know 1,000 times more about network marketing success than the naysayers. Successful people will encourage you with their words. They will give you ideas you can use to be successful. When you see people who have made it, it will help you realize that you can make it too. You just have to do what they did – and keep doing it until you get there too.

You Can Make Excuses or You Can Make Money

I recently had dinner with a judge who said he rarely sentenced a person who thought he was guilty. They all blamed other people, their circumstances, the cops or the system for their wrongdoing. It's so easy to make excuses.

You'll never make money if you keep making excuses for yourself. Nobody cares about your excuses, and you are only hurting yourself.

Just follow the successful people. Learn what they know. Do what they are doing. You'll make money.

Why Some Network Marketers Succeed

Successful network marketers have a plan to succeed.

When you went to school, you had a plan to succeed. You went to class every day, you listened to the teacher, you did your homework, and you studied for your tests.

If you continued through to the end, you graduated. That is the plan to succeed when you're in school.

Success doesn't come by luck. You have to plan for it, and you have to follow your plan. You have to say no to the things that will derail you from your success plan. It takes discipline and self-sacrifice to be successful, but the reward is well worth it when you are following the right plan.

"No pain no gain" is as true in network marketing as it is in anything else. It's just that the gain far outweighs the pain for those who take the success path in their businesses.

Recently I was visiting Nashville, Tennessee, the capital of country music. Many famous (and very rich) music stars and industry executives live in an exclusive suburb, which is one of the wealthiest cities in Tennessee. My friend Mike was driving me around the city. When we came near the area, he asked me, "Do you know what the richest man in that city does?"

I assumed he would give me the name of a famous music star or music executive.

Mike answered his own question. "He got his wealth through network marketing."

Successful network marketers immerse themselves in the training.

Successful people know they have to learn what it takes to succeed. Then they have to do it.

There is no network marketing gene. Nobody was born with network marketing skills. They are skills that everybody has to learn. True, some are better at the skills than others, but anyone can learn them. You can learn them.

There are at least 4 ways to acquire the skills. You need to take advantage of all of them.

Factors in Your Success

1. Your company's training

All network marketing companies offer training for their distributors. Not only does their training include general success skills for network marketers, but it also includes product knowledge and training as to how to present their products and services.

Get on the conference calls (you DO have unlimited long distance on your phone, don't you?). Get on the webinars. Read the training materials and go through all the training on the web site. Go to the training meetings and the conventions. This is your life we're talking about, and how you're going to live it for your entire future. Take responsibility for it. Take it seriously and invest in yourself. Investing in yourself is the best investment you can possibly make.

Pay special attention to the things the most successful people in your company are doing to build their businesses. When you go to your company's convention, seek some of them out and ask them about the most important things they did to achieve their level of success.

2. Your upline mentor (normally your sponsor)

Your upline mentor is a valuable resource for you. Not only can your mentor train you in the basics as you get started, but, if you're on a good team, he or she will help you recruit your first few people, will encourage and help you through the rough spots, and will always help you know the next things you will need to do in order to make it on your own in the business.

Also, take notes on the way your mentor is helping you, because in a matter of weeks or months, you will need to be the upline mentor for people on your own team.

3. Practice from doing

You learn what to do from the training. You learn to be good at it by practice. You get your practice by going to work every day, talking to people and making presentations.

Don't worry if you're not any good at it at first. We were all lousy at first. It is only as we continue to put our training into practice that we will become skillful network marketers.

4. Third-party books, CDs, seminars, etc.

Commitment to continual improvement is the key to reaching our potential and being successful.
--Dr. John Maxwell

What do you listen to when you are in the car, in the shower, and when you are getting dressed in the morning? Are you using that time to learn more about becoming the successful person you can become? Are you training your mind to look for and develop opportunities to advance in your business?

How to Be a Network Marketing Millionaire

Listen to good training and motivational speakers as much as you can. You already have the time to do it. That's because you can do it while you are doing other things that don't require too much of your attention.

Successful network marketers are successful because they don't do it their own way

There is another reason some network marketers are successful. They don't do it their own way. They learn the way that successful people do it, and they follow them.

It makes sense. When you learn what made other people successful, and when you do the same things, you will get the same results.

J. Paul Getty was the richest man in the world when I was growing up. He had made his fortune in the oil industry. One day a person came up to him and asked, "Mr. Getty, is there a formula I can follow to become wealthy like you?"

"Yes", answered Getty. "It's a very simple formula. If you follow it, I can guarantee you will get rich."

"What is it?" the man asked eagerly.

"There are just 3 things you have to do," replied the billionaire. "First, go to work early in the morning – every morning. Second, continue working late – after everyone else has finished for the day, And third, strike oil."

OK, you probably can't do what J. Paul Getty did. But you can develop the habits and do the things that made other people successful in network marketing. The skills you learn as you climb to the top in this industry can be far more profitable than an MBA from Harvard Business School.

Successful network marketers allocate the time to do their business every week.

Do you work a 9-5 job? If you do, is there any question as to where you'll be at 9:00 on Monday morning? Or Tuesday? Or your other work days? Why not? Because those are your work hours.

If you get home at 5:30 and have dinner at 6:00, what are you doing from 7:00 to 9:00 PM? And what about Saturday morning?

Working 9-5 on your job can make you a living, but it's what you do from 7-9 PM on your network marketing business that can make you a fortune.

If you want to be successful in your network marketing business, you need to schedule the hours you will be working and stick to them – just like you do on your job.

If you do that, you won't have to do it for more than a few years. Get your family on board and help them understand that, just because you are not at your job during your network marketing work time, it doesn't mean you are not at work. You are. And this is the work that is going to free up your time in a few years so you'll have a lot more time – and money – to devote to them.

Don't neglect your family. Schedule some time for them, because they are the most important people in your life. Where are you going to get the time for all that? Maybe it's time to turn the TV off and put your hobbies on hold for a while, so you can focus your life on the most important things.

A lot of network marketers find the best times for their work are evenings and Saturday mornings, and the best times for their families are Saturday afternoons and evenings, and Sundays after church.

Successful network marketers work every day.

There's a difference between going to work and actually working. A lot of people are very busy, but they never get anything accomplished.

A young man lost his job and went to the government office to apply for unemployment. He filled out the form and went to the window to turn it in. The man at the window asked him, "Did you register for work?"

"No," the young man answered.

"Then you need to go to Room 12 and register for work before I can process your application."

In Room 12, the young man was taken to a cubicle to register for work. The lady at the desk looked up and said, "Young man, do you want to work"?

"Heck no," he replied. "I don't want to work. I just want a job!"

You might laugh, but a lot of network marketers are not accomplishing anything when they are busy. The reason? They are not doing the things that are productive for building their businesses. Are you?

Successful network marketers work when they don't feel like working.

When the alarm goes off on Monday morning, do you really feel like getting up out of that comfortable bed and going to work? Probably not. Most people don't.

What do you do? You get up and go to work – even when you don't feel like it. If you stayed up too late the night before, if you have a headache or a cold, you still get up and go to work. You do it because you want to keep your job. Right?

When the time comes to go to work in your network marketing business, what do you do? Especially when you don't feel like working? What do you do when you don't feel like picking up the phone and calling that prospect, or going to that meeting?

Treat it like your job. It's more important than your job. Your job isn't going to give you residual income for life. Your job won't enable you to retire or semi-retire on a 6-figure income in a few years. Your network marketing business will, if you give it the attention it deserves.

Successful network marketers are successful because they don't quit.

A millionaire network marketer concluded his speech at his company's convention. The crowd roared with applause. As he stepped off the stage, a new distributor met him and asked him, "When you were just starting, did you ever feel like quitting?"

"Every day," was the reply. But I have a million-dollar income for one reason. I didn't quit."

Quitters never win. Winners never quit, Even when they feel like it.

I heard the story of an Olympic swimmer who wanted to swim from the California coast to Catalina Island – a distance of 26 miles. Usually when a swimmer attempts that type of swim, they have someone follow in a boat, just in case they have any trouble.

Shortly after she started, the fog rolled in, and she could not see where she was going, but she continued on. After many hours, she had no idea as to the remaining distance to the island.

She was very weary, and finally signaled to the boat that she wanted to stop.

Almost immediately after she was pulled into the boat the fog lifted and she could see Catalina. She quit just a few hundred feet before reaching the island!

It's always too soon to quit. You never know how close you are to the breakthrough you need to get you to the lifestyle you've always dreamed about.

As one convention speaker emphasized, Don't quit before the blessing!

Remember: If other people can succeed, so can you. They didn't succeed by quitting. Neither will you.

Treat it Like a Job!

We say that network marketing is not a job, but in one very important way, it IS a job.

It is not a job. You don't have to report to the office every day and do what your boss tells you to do. You are your boss.

It is a job. You have to work just as hard as you do on your job – or harder. You do have a boss. The boss is you. You

need to determine what you must do, and you need to do it. If you don't follow your boss's directives at your day job, you will get fired. If you don't set the course for your business and follow it, you will fail in your business. There is no reason to fail. Your upline mentor will help you set the course, and your job is to stay on it until you achieve the lifestyle of your dreams.

Why Some Fail and Others Succeed

Remember, it's not net-sit marketing. It's netWORK marketing! There is a reason the word work is in there.

Network marketers fail for the same reasons that some students fail, employees fail, and other businesspeople fail. Others enjoy success for the same reasons that people in other careers and businesses succeed. They do the things that bring success, and they develop habits of success.

6 How to Choose a Network Marketing Company

The Track Record of the Company

It's always safer to join a company that has a proven track record. They have been in the business for a number of years, and they have survived the experimental stages and the growing pains of a new company.

Most new businesses fail in the first 5 years. That is even more common with new network marketing companies. If you join a company that is less than 5 years old, the company has a high risk of going under and carrying you down with it – even if you are successful in the company.

Even older, more established companies can be a problem. Getting into the wrong company can end in disaster, even if you make it to the top. That happened to me.

Until recently I was with a network marketing company that was owned by a couple of aging brothers who had no accountability in the way they ran the company. They were very impulsive, and sometimes they made major changes in company policy on a whim during their afternoon coffee at Starbucks.

As they reached their mid-60's they began to look for ways to take our residual income away from us. That caused the company to go into a deep decline. Then, on a whim, they terminated 900 of us in one day because they didn't want to pay us any more. It cost me millions of dollars in residual income that I earned and should have been getting paid for the rest of my life.

During my tenure with the company I earned a lot of money and learned a lot about network marketing skills. That's why I'm able to write this book. Although it left me in bad financial shape, I got a great education which is causing me to rise again.

Look for a stable company with good management, a strong vision for the future and the flexibility to change with technological advancement and market conditions.

Pre-Launches and Ground Floor Opportunities

Pre-Launches and Ground Floor Opportunities are a big gamble. An article on eHow.com quoted SBA government statistics that showed 56% of all new businesses close their doors forever before their fifth anniversary. If you join a company that is less than 5 years old, you have a 56% chance of being forced out of business by your company's failure. Do you really want to take that risk?

"That doesn't apply to our company," they say. "We're strong and growing like crazy!" Remember, that's what they all said before they went under. The Titanic was unsinkable, too.

If you join a company less than 5 years old, there is a 56% chance your company will fail and you will lose everything.

How to Choose a Network Marketing Company

Often a new company will start recruiting people before they are selling products or services. They call it a *Pre-Launch.*

This is a tactic that some cash-strapped companies do to start a network marketing company. They use the cash generated from the pre-launch (hopefully) to start their companies. They will swear up and down that they are not doing it to raise cash, but it's probably not true. Some owners have tried to disappear with the cash they raised from the pre-launch. I know a lot of people who have lost money from pre-launches and start-up companies. I did too, before I knew any better.

They will dangle all kinds of carrots in front of you to get you to join. Some of these carrots are:

- Join for half off
- Thousands of people coming in will be placed under you
- You can get extra bonuses when you build your team
- The people on the "ground floor" are the ones who will be the richest.

Most pre-launches are nothing more than pre-failures. They are dead within 5 years or less. Most ground floor opportunities end up six feet under the ground.

Regardless what they tell you, most new companies are still trying to figure out how to be successful in the business, and you're their guinea pig.

The reward can be great, but for most people, the risk isn't worth it. And, the reward can be just as great or greater with an established company that has a successful track record.

If You Can't Resist the Temptation to Join an Unproven Company

Find out who the founders, owners and corporate executives are. Check their reputations on Google. A lot of failed network marketing company owners or executives will reincarnate themselves a few years later with new networking "opportunities." Beware of these resurfaced failures. Some of them are even con artists.

1. Have they been involved in other network marketing companies before?
2. Did their previous company(ies) fail?
3. If they sold their company, who bought it, and how is it doing today?
4. Have they been involved in or suspected of criminal activity? (Many of them have).

Recently we tried to recruit some friends into our company. They were going to join. Then they joined a new company that is supposed to give people a rebate on their gasoline purchases. They sent an enthusiastic email to introduce their new company. It all looked fishy to me. After a quick search on Google I saw the founder of the new company had done a similar company – a scam – about 10 years earlier. A lot of people who joined that company lost money – including me.

Another friend contacted us last week about a new company she had joined. I Googled the founders and discovered they had a checkered background in Europe.

How to Choose a Network Marketing Company

It is amazing how many new network marketing companies are being started by people with undesirable backgrounds. They get away with it because they know how to use hype to build a big following. They don't have long term goals for their companies. Their plan is to make a big money grab and then disappear for a while. Then they come back.

Fortunately, it is easy to check people out online quickly – most of the time. Don't listen to what these people and their devotees say about themselves. You need to see what they did, and what third-party evidence you can find.

If you still decide to "roll the dice" and join an unproven company like this, realize it's like buying a lottery ticket. You could win big. Most likely, however, you will lose your money – and your credibility with the people you share the business with.

Sunrise Industry or Sunset Industry

In the 1880's to the early 1900's, my great grandfather supported his family by making buggies in Hamilton, Ontario, Canada. He painstakingly hand-crafted each buggy. He even made the wheels and the leather seats. His industry was about to die. While he was still making  buggies, many budding industrialists were experimenting with making cars just 200 miles away in Detroit.

He saw the handwriting on the wall, he closed up shop, sold his house and moved to Detroit to work in the car industry. (That's why I'm American and not Canadian).

Is the company you are considering in an industry that has a strong future? Is your company able to change with the times? The business climate is changing faster than at any time in history. Entire industries will be wiped out and replaced by other industries. Pick an industry with a strong future.

Twenty years ago, there were two large network marketing companies selling long distance phone services. That was in the days when it cost 25¢ a minute to make a long distance call, and it was possible to make money selling long distance services.

As the industry changed, both companies began to look for other ways to keep making money. One of the companies made the transition successfully. The other one didn't.

You want to make sure you are in a company that is in a stable, growing industry, and that is able to adapt quickly enough to changing trends within that industry.

Is it a Recession-Proof Industry?

I don't want to sound like a prophet of doom, but the US government has borrowed and overspent so much money that it will likely be difficult to have the level of prosperity we have enjoyed in the near future, if ever. At this writing, the economies of several European countries are on life support, or almost there, so many other countries are facing similar problems. That means many industries will suffer. Will yours?

When people aren't making enough money, or they are afraid they won't be, they change their spending habits and cut a lot of things out of their budgets – including many of the things sold by a lot of network marketing companies.

With the bad economy, there are many people who have stopped going to movies. They stay home and watch TV or rent a

DVD instead. Many people have cut back on eating out, or they go to cheaper restaurants. A friend who manages a McDonald's told me he is getting a lot of customers who used to eat at the more expensive restaurants, but with the bad economy they are eating cheaper fast food instead.

So, what does this mean to you when you are looking for a network marketing company to join?

If the products are expensive, they will be harder to sell when people are experiencing hard times. If people can do without them, many will stop buying them. Or they will be going to Wal-Mart to look for cheaper alternatives.

Recession-proof network marketing companies are those that market products that people need, and that they can't get a cheaper brand at the store. Sure, your products might be better quality, but that's not the point – especially in a bad economy. A Cadillac is better than a Toyota, but a lot more people buy Toyotas. Many of them would rather be driving a Cadillac, but they either can't or won't spend the extra money for a better car.

Is the Product Optional or Essential?

If your company is marketing optional products or services, you are selling something that most people will do without when the going gets tough – or when they decide to do other things with their money. If you're selling vitamins, health drinks or other things that most people don't feel they need, they know very well they can live without them. A weight loss product, on the other hand, would be considered essential, not for everybody, but for large numbers of overweight people.

Is the Product a Consumable Product?

What if you could sell water filter machines and make $200 per .sale in a network marketing company? You and your downline would have to be constantly selling a lot of water machines, because people don't buy them that often, and most people don't see the need to buy them at all, even though you may think they're very necessary.

Consumable products or services, on the other hand, are the things that people buy over and over – usually every month. That means, when you or your downline makes a sale, you get paid over and over for that sale, because you have repeat business.

Kinds of Consumables

1. Repeat Purchase

A repeat purchase consumable is the type where a customer has to make repeat decisions to purchase again and again. It's easy for the customer to stop buying at any time.

2. Autoship

Many companies have tried to get around this by offering an autoship program, in which a customer automatically gets a shipment – and his credit card gets charged automatically – every month. Most of the autoship products are expensive - $50 to $100 a month or more. Whenever the UPS man arrives with the product, customers are automatically reminded that they are paying every month.

3. Membership

A membership type service is also delivered and billed automatically every month, but it is more inconvenient for a customer to decide to quit. Membership services would include anything that is not physically delivered to customers.

The Product Quadrant

"Before we build a better mousetrap,
we need to find out if there are any mice out there."

--Yogi Berra

The Product Quadrant

	Essential	Optional
Consumable	**1** Essential Consumable	**2** Optional Consumable
Non-Consumable	**3** Essential Non-Consumable	**4** Optional Non-Consumable

©2011 Bob Sharpe

For ease of communication we are going to include both products and services under the label Product in this section.

Every product you can sell in network marketing is either Essential or Optional, and every product is also Consumable or Non-Consumable.

Essential products are the easiest to sell, as long as they are competitively priced. An essential product is one that people are going to buy – either from you or from someone else, so you might as well get the sale. Consumable products are the ones that generate repeat income.

Essential products, by the way, are the products that the customers consider to be essential – not the products you think are essential when you are trying to market them.

By looking at the quadrant, it is obvious that the products in the First Quadrant have the most income potential for the least amount of work. That is because they are both easy to sell

(Essential) and they provide an automatic repeat income (Consumable.). The Quadrant 4 products are the most difficult to make a living – or a fortune – with because they are harder to sell (Optional) and they are a one-time purchase (Non-Consumable)..

A Quadrant 2 network marketing opportunity is good if you happen to know a lot of people who feel your products are essential, but the product will be harder to sell to everyone else. Also, many network marketing companies have products that fit into more than one Quadrant.

You are always better off in a company that markets products and services in Quadrant 1 or possibly Quadrant 2 – even if you really love the products from another quadrant.

The Third World Country Effect

Some network marketing companies take pride in the fact that their top earners earn $1,000,000 a year – or even $1,000,000 a month. So what? Do you think you'll ever earn that kind of money in one of those companies? Probably not. But what if you could make $500,000 a year?

Some of these companies are like third world countries. Here's what I mean…

Many third world countries have a very small middle class, if any. There are a few extremely wealthy people at the top, and they're getting richer all the time. They own the big industries, and often they're in cahoots with their governments. The overwhelming majority of the citizenry, however, is very poor. And the rich keep getting more money at the expense of the poor.

Nobody would ever think Somalia is a prosperous country – even if the richest person in the country is a billionaire.

Some network marketing companies, likewise, have a few very wealthy people at the top. And they're getting richer all the time. All the people at the bottom are contributing to their wealth by buying expensive products in the hope that they, too, will make money someday. The rich in these companies get richer, while the poor get poorer.

Companies with a Strong "Middle Class"

The true test of a great network marketing company is not how much money the top people are making. It's how many people are making a good living in the company – a good middle class. How many people are making a full-time income of, $50,000 to $150,000 a year?

When VarTec Communications, the parent company of the defunct network marketing company Excel Communications failed in 2004, I read in the Dallas paper that out of 108,000 distributors, only 99 - 0.09% - were making as much as $1,000 a month – and that's not a full-time income! (The top guy was making about $3,000,000 a year, I think). Regardless of what Excel claimed in their opportunity meetings, they did not have a middle class. They were like a third world country, because very few of their people were able to make a decent full-time living.

I prefer a Quadrant 1 company with a very strong middle class. I like to see a company where a lot of people who are earning substantial full-time incomes. I also like to see a strong upper class of people who are making multiple 6-figure incomes and more.

Unless you are a super-achiever who is used to earning $500,000 a year or more in network marketing, forget about what the top earners are making in the company you are considering. Look at the middle class earners in the company. How many are there? What does it take to get there?

Industry Leader or "Me Too" Company?

Do you remember the Daihatsu, the Daewoo or the Yugo? (In case you don't remember, those were cars imported to the US over the past 30 years or so). When they first arrived, people didn't know about them. They did know about Fords and Chevys. When they came out, do you think it would be as easy to sell them as it would be to sell Fords and Chevrolets?

Why is that? Fords and Chevrolets were the industry leaders. For everybody who bought a Daihatsu, there were 1,000 or more people buying Fords and Chevrolets. That meant two things:

1. Fords and Chevrolets were easier to sell, so you would naturally sell more of them;
2. Ford and Chevrolet were better established brands, so the chances were your job would be more stable in the future.

Once you have selected a Quadrant 1 product, look for the companies that are the network marketing industry leaders for those products. In many cases an industry leader will be one of your best choices.

The Compensation Plan

Here are some questions you should consider:

1. How difficult is it to understand and explain the compensation plan to others?

2. Exactly what must I do to earn back my startup investment? Will it be difficult to earn it back in the first month?

3. What do I have to do to qualify for overrides from the business my downline puts on?

4. How many levels deep does the company pay overrides on?

5. What will it take to reach the $300 a month residual income level? How soon can an average person make it?

6. What will I need to do to make a full-time living in the company? If I work hard and follow the company's success plan, how long can I expect it to take? How difficult will it be to do it in my first year?

7. Does the company have a habit of changing the compensation plan often?

How Do You Feel About the Products or Services?

Do you have to love the product or service you are selling to be successful? No, you have to believe in the product, but you don't have to be in love with it.

You have to believe it is a great product at a fair price. You have to be confident that people genuinely benefit from buying and using it. You do not have to be absolutely enamored with it. Your network marketing business is your job, and your job is to market good products and recruit people into a business that pays you well.

Be a Businessperson, not an Evangelist

If your network marketing business is your platform to be an evangelist for a product you love, you may not do well if it is not a Quadrant 1 product. I've seen many network marketers who were so passionate about their products they lost site of the business and why they were in it.

Network marketing is a professional business. You are in business to make money by supplying products and services that make peoples' lives better.

My dad's best friend Bill decided – in his early 20's – that he wanted to be rich. He started a screw machine company in the Detroit area. After a decade of working hard, he achieved his goal. I remember walking through his factory when I was a kid and wondering what all that stuff was that they were making.

As his wealth grew, he bought a big house in an exclusive suburb, he bought a beautiful boat, and he lived a very nice lifestyle. He passed away in his late 70's. Several years after he died, his widow told my mother that there was no way she could spend money as fast as she was making it from their investments

Was Bill in love with the screw machine parts he was manufacturing? Heck no. He was in love with the opportunity he found to make money. He had seen an opportunity to make a lot of money by making boring stuff that other companies needed, and he capitalized on that opportunity.

I know for a fact that there were a lot of things and people in Bill's life that he loved more than the stuff his factory was turning out. It was only a means to a very important end.

He did a good job, he provided an important service at a fair price, and he got rich. He was in love with what his business could do for him and his family. That's what motivated him.

The most important thing in your network marketing business is what it can do for you, your family, your customers and your downline. The product is only the vehicle to make it happen.

Are there network marketing products that you really, really love? Great. If they're not overpriced, use them. If they're not Quadrant 1 products, don't sell them. Get into a Quadrant 1 network marketing business. After all, your income and lifestyle are far more important than any wonderful product could possibly be.

If you really love a non-Quadrant 1 network marketing product, you might join the business so you can get the products cheaper. If you know some other people who would really love the products, you might share them, and eventually your beloved products might pay for themselves, but don't worry if they don't, because the money is in Quadrant 1.

Focus on your Quadrant 1 business; because that's the easiest and fastest way you are going to achieve the lifestyle of your dreams.

Going back to my dad's friend Bill - he loved his home more than he loved his screw machine parts, but he wasn't selling houses. He loved his Cadillac better than his screw machine parts, but he wasn't selling Cadillacs, and he loved his family more than anything. He was making and selling screw machine parts so that he and his family could afford and enjoy the stuff they loved.

Will the Products or Services Sell on Their Own Merit?

Many products that are sold through network marketing companies are so expensive that very few people would buy them if they didn't think they would be able to make money with them. Those are the products don't sell on their own merit.

If your network marketing vitamins cost 3 times as much as the vitamins at Costco, they'd better be 3 times as good. They might be better than the Costco vitamins, but are they really 3 times better? Who said so? How do you know? How many independent experts – who are not connected with the company – agree?

"But," you say, "My company's health products are the best in the world."

Really? How do you know that? Again, who said so? A company spokesperson, or an independent expert?

"Because my company has a doctor or a biochemist who says they are."

So what! There are at least 100 other companies that claim the same thing, and that have the same "proof." It's just a matter that you chose to believe your company instead of all the others.

So much of that "reasoning" goes on that many network marketers and their companies have lost credibility in the marketplace. If you're doing that kind of marketing, you have to convince people of the unique merits of your product before you can sell them, and for many people, it's a very hard sell.

Wouldn't it be easier if you were marketing a product that didn't take convincing? You can completely eliminate one difficult step in building your business.

How to Choose a Network Marketing Company

Selling products that take convincing is like trying to push a car uphill. Selling a product that doesn't take convincing is like pushing a car downhill. If you had the choice of pushing uphill or pushing downhill, which would you rather do?

Are You Required to Buy a Lot of Products?

Some companies encourage or even require distributors to purchase a lot of product before they sell it. This is called frontloading Frontloading is an indicator that the company could be an illegal pyramid scheme.

Some companies offer you the opportunity to buy more than one "position" or distributorship to either operate yourself or to sell to a person you recruit. Companies that do this are illegal. I was in the process of joining one about 20 years ago – before I knew any better. The day I was planning to go to a meeting and join the company I got a call from my prospective sponsor. She told me not to join, because she had just gotten word that the company was under investigation by the Federal Trade Commission. Within two weeks the company was shut down by the Government for frontloading.

What Happens With Some Companies

Why didn't your upline tell you this would happen? © 2002, Bob Sharpe

How to Tell if a Company is a Pyramid Scheme

"But wait," someone says. Aren't all network marketing companies pyramids?

It all depends how you define a pyramid. Yes, all network marketing companies have a pyramid shaped structure. But then, so do all companies. Ford Motor Company has a guy at the top, some elite people under him, others under them, and so on, until you get the guys at the bottom who clean the bathrooms in the factories. That's also a pyramid business. So is Disney. So is Microsoft. So is the company you work for.

It doesn't matter what business or organizations you're talking about, the people at the top make more money than the people at the bottom. They also contribute more to the profitability of the organization than the people at the bottom, so they deserve more pay.

Definition of Pyramid Schemes

This explanation is rather long, but it explains what they are. Once you see this, it becomes obvious that legitimate network market companies are not pyramid schemes, although some pyramid schemes pose as legitimate network marketing companies.

One of the functions of The Federal Trade Commission (FTC) is to regulate business opportunities and to shut down the scams. I found this definition of a pyramid scheme from a speech given by their General Counsel to the International Monetary Fund on their web site:

www.ftc.gov/speeches/other/dvimf16.shtm

I figured it would be an authoritative definition. If you don't want to read the whole thing, read the underlined sentences. (Emphasis mine).

PREPARED STATEMENT OF
DEBRA A. VALENTINE, GENERAL COUNSEL FOR
THE U.S. FEDERAL TRADE COMMISSION
on
"PYRAMID SCHEMES"
presented at the
INTERNATIONAL MONETARY FUND'S
SEMINAR ON CURRENT LEGAL ISSUES AFFECTING
CENTRAL BANKS
Washington, D.C.
May 13, 1998

. . . Pyramid schemes now come in so many forms that they may be difficult to recognize immediately. However, they all share one overriding characteristic. They promise consumers or investors large profits based primarily on recruiting others to join their program, not based on profits from any real investment or real sale of goods to the public. Some schemes may purport to sell a product, but they often simply use the product to hide their pyramid structure. There are two tell-tale signs that a product is simply being used to disguise a pyramid scheme: inventory loading and a lack of retail sales. Inventory loading occurs when a company's incentive program forces recruits to buy more products than they could ever sell, often at inflated prices. If this occurs throughout the company's distribution system, the people at the top of the pyramid reap substantial profits, even though little or no product moves to market. The people at the bottom make excessive payments for inventory that simply accumulates in their basements. A lack of retail sales is also a red flag that a pyramid exists. Many pyramid schemes will claim that their product is selling like hot cakes. However, on closer examination, the sales occur only between people inside the pyramid structure or to new recruits joining the structure, not to consumers out in the general public.

A Ponzi scheme is closely related to a pyramid because it revolves around continuous recruiting, but in a Ponzi scheme the promoter generally has no product to sell and pays no commission to investors who recruit new "members." Instead, the promoter collects payments from a stream of people, promising them all the same high rate of return on a short-term investment. In the typical Ponzi scheme, there is no real investment opportunity, and the promoter just uses the money from new recruits to pay obligations owed to longer-standing members of the program. . . .

Both Ponzi schemes and pyramids are quite seductive because they may be able to deliver a high rate of return to a few early investors for a short period of time. Yet, both pyramid and Ponzi schemes are illegal because they inevitably must fall apart. No program can recruit new members forever. Every pyramid or Ponzi scheme collapses because it cannot expand beyond the size of the earth's population. When the scheme collapses, most investors find themselves at the bottom, unable to recoup their losses. . . .

How to Choose a Network Marketing Company

Legitimate network marketing programs differ from pyramid schemes in the following ways:

1. Legitimate network marketing companies have a legitimate product or service to sell

2. They pay commissions on the sale of products, not on the recruiting of distributors.

3. The only way distributors make money from recruiting is by overriding the product or service sales of the distributors recruited and the personal sales of the recruits.

4. Anyone can make a substantial income if they recruit and build an organization that sells a lot of products or services.

7 How to Choose Your Upline Team

Now that you've chosen a company, it's time to decide who will be your upline. This is very important. Your upline team is a major factor in your success in the company. Many network marketing failures could have succeeded had they had good upline support.

Your upline team and the support they provide can mean the difference between having a million-dollar career and failure. Read this statement over and over again. It is that important.

> **Your upline team and the support they provide can mean the difference between having a million-dollar career and failure.**

A good upline team will provide you with training, motivation, accountability, mentoring, recognition any help you need to become successful in the business. Upline leaders know that their success is dependent on the success of their downlines, and they invest a lot of time and money in helping the people in their organizations to become successful leaders.

Importance of a good team leader

A team leader is a person who is well advanced in the business and is making a sizeable income. The team leader of the organization you will be joining may have a downline of hundreds or thousands of people, so he or she may be too busy to work with you personally. That's OK, as long as you will have a successful and knowledgeable person in your upline to mentor you.

Here's how effective team leaders help their downlines:

1. A team training web site where all downline members can get training.

2. A team blog or email blast with training help.

3. Team conference calls or webinars or podcasts to keep people trained, motivated and up-to-date on company news and events.

4. Team meetings at the corporate conventions after (not during) the company's sessions to train, motivate and give recognition.

5. Mastermind session conference calls for team members to share challenges and solutions.

6. Special recognition for team members who reach important milestones in their network marketing businesses.

Before you join a company, find out who your team leader will be, and what they are doing to support their downline. Do not join under a team that does not have a supportive leader. When you join, take advantage of all the support your team offers.

Upline Mentor

You will need someone to mentor you while you are starting out. Normally your sponsor – the person who recruited you into the business – will be your upline mentor. If your

sponsor is inexperienced or is unwilling, you will need someone else in your upline to be your mentor.

Your mentor is the person who is responsible to help you get started in the business successfully. A good upline mentor can help you be successful quickly. Make sure you will have an upline mentor who meets these qualifications, and who will work with you to get you started.

Don't expect your upline mentor to do your work for you. He or she won't make calls for you, but they will make calls with you. Be careful to not waste their time. Get good solid prospects to contact with them.

Also, don't expect your upline mentor to continue making your calls with you forever. The purpose of your mentor is to duplicate himself in you, so you in turn can be the upline mentor for your people, and so you can train your people to be upline mentors for the people they recruit. That is how your business will multiply.

Upline mentor job description and responsibility to you:

1. Spend time with you to help you be successful
2. Help you recruit your first 3 downline distributors in your first 30 days with 3-way calls and/or personal visits.
3. Answer questions and help you always to know what to do next to build your business.
4. Hold you accountable for the things you need to do to move forward your first month or so.

If the person who is trying to recruit you into the business is too new to mentor you, that's OK – as long as there is a successful person in their upline who is willing to mentor you.

Before you join a networking business, ask your prospective sponsor who will be your upline mentor and what they will do to help you. This is one of the most important considerations in choosing your network marketing opportunity.

Dr. Lee Roberson was famous for saying, "Everything rises and falls on leadership." You want to be close enough to the right kind of leadership that will help you rise to the top in the business. It's a business decision. *Your future lifestyle depends on it.*

Your upline mentor could be a team leader at the top of the company's compensation plan. Or he or she might be several levels under that leader, but still very successful in the business.

It's an undeniable fact. Your chances for success will increase immensely if you are part of a successful team and you have a successful mentor. That's why professional baseball teams spend millions of dollars to hire the best coaches they can. The coaches are mentoring and training the players to improve their game.

8 Government Help to Finance Your Business

Look, we play, "The Star Spangled Banner" before every game.
You want us to pay income taxes too?
--Bill Veeck, former owner of the
Cleveland Indians and Chicago White Sox

 Great news! If you are in the US, you stand a good chance of being eligible for financial help from the Government for your business. In fact, if you are eligible, you can very likely get enough financial help from the Government to totally reimburse you for the costs of starting and running your business.

Disclaimer: I am not an accountant or a tax professional. I cannot give tax advice. This section is to make you aware of the financial incentives the US Government makes available to you to build your home business.

For specific advice, consult an accountant who specializes in home based businesses. Most accountants are not too familiar with this specialty and may not be able to help you much. You wouldn't go to a podiatrist for a heart problem, even if he is the best podiatrist in town. Likewise, don't go to an accountant who doesn't have a deep knowledge of the special needs and incentives for home based businesses.

Note to people outside the US: This section specifically applies to network marketers in the United States. Many other countries have similar laws. Read this and then consult a professional in your own country to see what program they have that you can take advantage of.

No, Uncle Sam is not going to write you a check to start or run your business. He will do the next best thing, however.

Probably at least 70-80% of network marketers qualify to get extra money through this government program every month – starting this month.

How it works:

1. People with legitimate home-based businesses qualify for more legitimate tax deductions than any other class of people in the U.S. Many network marketers can legally use these deductions to reduce their State and Federal income tax liability by $4,000 or more per year.
2. That means you will have less tax to pay on April 15.
3. If you have a regular job, your employer won't have to deduct as much from your paycheck to satisfy your tax obligation in April.
4. Therefore you are legally entitled to rework your W4 form to lower the amount of taxes your employer will have to deduct each payday.
5. *Voila!* There you have it. An instant raise in your take home pay every payday as long as you continue working your network marketing business.

With a financial incentive like this, you can't afford to quit your business!

How it will Help You if You Are Self-Employed

Do you remember those quarterly payments you have to make to the IRS? When you claim your deductions, you won't have to pay as much each quarter. What would it feel like if you could cut $500, $1,000 or more each quarter?

How much extra money will you get every month? It depends on a lot of things, including your income, the number of deductions you get now, and the amount of tax money already being deducted from your paycheck.

It is not uncommon for people to get an extra $200 to $400 per month. This money is 100% yours. It's after-tax money, so you won't have to pay taxes on it. You've already paid the taxes on it.

Warning: Don't redo your W4 form unless you know how much to change it. You need to do it correctly. Go to the Resource section of www.ITrainMillionaires.com first. The book there has a worksheet and a formula so you know exactly what to do to do it right. It's not difficult, but you need to follow the rules and stick to the formula.

Some of the things you can deduct

1. Part of your rent or mortgage payment
2. Part of your utility bills
3. Part of your phone bill
4. Part of your Internet cost
5. Part of the cost of your computer hardware
6. The cost of your business-related software
7. 51¢ for every business mile you drive (as of 2011)
8. 50% of every restaurant meal when you conduct business at the meal
9. All of the other normal costs of doing your business

10. The cost of going to your company's meetings and conventions
11. The cost of training and motivational tapes, CDs and mp3s to keep you trained and motivated in your business
12. The cost of this book – if you are in network marketing.

Why Does the Government Do This?

It stimulates the Economy

New businesses stimulate the economy by making and spending more money, which, in turn, creates jobs and overall prosperity.

It helps reduce unemployment

The people who are successful at creating new businesses are creating jobs. When you become successful and quit your job, that's one more job available for another person to take.

It creates more taxable income

You are paying less in tax now, but guess what happens when you quadruple your income? You'll be paying more taxes – even after all the great deductions you are getting. Hmmm… Uncle Sam is pretty smart after all, isn't he?

Keep your receipts and document all your expenses.

I keep an envelope in the pocket in my car door. Every time I get a tax-deductible receipt, I put it in the envelope. When the envelope gets full, I empty it into a tax file folder in my file cabinet. That way I have everything I need at tax time.

Government Help to Finance Your Business

One of my colleagues has a book and a program to help network marketers claim all the legitimate tax deductions the Government is willing to give them.

You can get more information in the Resource section of www.ITrainMillionaires.com.

Why You Need to Do This

1. Don't leave money on the table when it is available to you.
2. It gives you more money to invest in your business which you can use to advertise and go to your company's conventions, which, in turn, will increase your income.
3. Whenever you get discouraged and think about quitting, think of the money it will cost you if you have to give up your tax deductions.

Why You Need to Share This

1. It helps you recruit more people, because it takes the risk out of joining your company.
2. Most network marketers don't know about this, so when you present it to a prospect, you have more to offer them when they join you instead of someone else.
3. It aids retention. People are less likely to quit when they realize it will cost them money to quit.

What to Do Next

Get the information from the Resources section of

www.ITrainMillionaires.com

There is a link there to the best home-based business tax savings program I have ever found. They have regular webinars and conference calls, and they sell a book that gives you all the information you need to take all the tax deductions you are legally entitled to if you are a US taxpayer.

9 Starting Out Right

Most of the successful people in network marketing started fast and never looked back. Well, that's only part true. Most of them failed in at least 1 or 2 other companies before they found a company they became successful in. If this is your first venture into network marketing, follow this book and your upline mentor, and you won't have to go through the failures we did.

That's my story, too, except for one detail. I failed in 16 different companies before I became a successful network marketer. I'm really glad I didn't quit. I always realized that if others could make it I could make it, and I kept plodding on until I found success. I'm really glad I did.

Your First 48-72 Hours

During your first 48-72 hours, you will be spending 80-90% of your time training and setting up, and 10-20% of your time contacting people.

Once you have completed this phase, you will be spending 20% of your time in training and 80% of your time contacting people and making presentations for your business.

What is your WHY?

1. What do you want to get out of your network marketing career?
2. When you get it, how will it change your life?
3. How important is it to you?
4. What are you willing to do to get it?
5. Do you believe you can really have it?

You don't have to settle for the best a job can offer. You want more, and you can have it. Your job won't offer you residual income that continues to grow every month. It won't give you the chance to have all the money you could ever want and all the time to enjoy it in just a few short years.

You spent years in school training for your job. Perhaps you spent tens of thousands of dollars, or even hundreds of thousands of dollars just for the education to have a job. And what will the job give you? A chance to work every day for 40 years so that you can pay the bills every month and maybe enjoy a few of the extras that life has to offer.

If you were willing to sacrifice a few years and thousands of dollars so you could have a job for 40 years, what would you be willing to sacrifice to be able to work for 5 years and be set for life? Your job won't do that for you.

How important is that to you?

OK, what do you want, and why do you want it?

If you want your life to change, you must do something to change it. Most people live their lives aimlessly, reacting to everything that comes along. They don't have a strategy to rise up and improve their lifestyles. They are going nowhere fast, except for getting older.

Why do you want to do this business? What do you want it to do for you?

Take some time and then write down your WHY. Someone once said, "If your Why doesn't make you cry, it isn't strong enough."

How do you want the quality of your life to change? Assuming you have your health, it all revolves around having enough time and money. If you had all of both you wanted or needed, what would you do?

- Get out of debt
- Spend more time with family
- Travel
- Volunteer with your church
- Pay for your kids' Christian school and college
- Help less fortunate people here and abroad
- Or????

Get your notebook out and write down your why.

What are your goals?

Give me a stock clerk with goals,
and I'll give you a men who will make history.
Give me a man without goals,
and I'll give you a stock clerk.
--J. C. Penney

Some people just want to supplement their income with $1,000 or $2,000 per month residual income. Others want wealth and total time freedom. Either one is OK. What are your goals?

Other things to do your first 48-72 hours

1. Ask your upline mentor if they have a contact list available for you. If not, make one. This list should including names, phone numbers and emails of
    a. Your sponsor
    b. Your upline mentor (if different from your sponsor)
    c. Your team leader
    d. Your company's Distributor Service Department
    e. Your company's IVR if they have one.
    f. The phone numbers, PIN numbers, dates and times of all of your company's and team's conference calls
2. Get unlimited long distance, voice mail and 3-way calling for your phone. (You can get landline phone service with

unlimited long distance and all the calling features for less than $25 a month) and you can keep your phone number.

3. Complete the forms for direct deposit of your paychecks if it is available from your company. You'll get paid faster, and some companies pay more often when they cay use direct deposit.

4. If your company has a personalized web site for you, sign up for it and familiarize yourself with it.

5. Make your Top 40 List – a list of 40 or more people to contact about your business who could become customers or downline distributors. Include their phone numbers and email addresses. Email it to your upline mentor.

6. Ask your upline mentor to make some 3-way calls with you to help recruit your prospects into your business.

7. If your company or upline team has any online training for new distributors, complete it.

8. Set up your schedule for working your business.

9. Set up a game plan interview with your upline mentor. Discuss your business work schedule and get help for the next things you need to do in your business.

Supplies to Get

1. 3-ring binder and dividers to keep the following:
   a. Scripts and presentations
   b. Schedules
   c. Product information
   d. Prospect lists
   e. Forms

2. 8½ x 11" spiral binder to keep chronological notes of everything you learn at trainings and conventions. Carry it with you to all these events and date all entries in the left-hand column.

3. Business cards

How to Be a Network Marketing Millionaire

Your Next 4 Weeks

Seventy percent of success in life is showing up.
--Woody Allen

Take advantage of all the training opportunities you have. Practice your presentation and give it as many times as you can. Develop the work habits that will bring you to success. Work on getting your first promotion during your first month.

The 48-Hour Rule

The fortune is in the follow up!

Whenever you make an initial contact with a prospect, always follow up within 48 hours whenever possible. If this is a person you have met for the first time, they will forget you fast if you don't follow up quickly.

The rule also applies to presentations. Many people will not join after the first presentation, but many will join if you follow up. Call them within 48 hours of the time you exposed them to a presentation, whether that presentation was by you, your upline mentor or in a business briefing or home meeting. 48 hours is the rule. Get 'em before they get away!

Remember, if they are looking at your business, there is a good chance they are looking at other businesses too. If somebody else is better at following up than you are, they will probably get them, and you'll lose out.

10 What it Takes to Work Your Business

Success is a choice. It's always your choice.
--Unknown

You don't make any money until you sell products or services, or you recruit new people who sell products or services. That means you must continually perform those activities to make money in the business. Sell. Recruit. Sell. Recruit.

When you get active in selling and recruiting you realize how important it is to have a Quadrant 1 product or service.

How Many Presentations do I Need to Make?

If you are working part-time in your business you should make at least one complete presentation per day.

If you are working full-time – you should make two to three complete presentations per day.

These could be product presentations to get customers, or they could be business opportunity presentations to recruit people for your downline.

You can do a lot of work in your business, but you won't make any money until you give presentations and gather customers and downline business partners who also gather customers.

How to Do a 3-Way Call with Your Upline Mentor

Before the call, edify your upline mentor. Tell your prospect how helpful and successful the mentor is (assuming he or she really is successful). Make your prospect feel that your upline mentor is well worth listening to.

Schedule the 3-way call in advance with your upline mentor at a time that is good for him.

Speak up then shut up

When you have both people on the line, introduce them and then shut up, unless one of them addresses you. Do not interrupt your upline mentor's speaking. Take notes so you will be able to help your people in the future.

Learn all you can from your mentor's presentation, because you will be doing them on your own soon, and soon after that you will be doing 3-way calls for your downline.

Harnessing the Amazing Power of Duplication

Network marketing works because of duplication. If you can learn a few simple skills, make a few sales and recruit a few people in your downline, you can show your new people how to do what you just did. That's duplication. Now if you help them to help their new people to do the same, that's duplication again. It's that simple. Duplication that duplicates over and over can build an amazing income over time.

By this time you'll have 10-20 or more people on your 3rd level. If you and the people on your 1st and 2nd levels support the 3rd level people to do the same, you'll have 80 to 100 people on your 4th level, even if nobody recruits a lot of people. Duplication produces multiplication, and multiplication produces exponential growth.

One network marketing leader gave me this example:

Let's assume you recruit 3 people and gather 3 customers. Then you go to work to help each of your 3 people to recruit 3 people, and each of them gathers just 3 customers.

"Repeat the process 8 times," the presenter told us, "and the results are amazing, because of the power of multiplication.

"On your 8th level, you'll have 6,561 distributors. If each one has 3 customers, you'll have 29,520 customers in your organization. In our company," he went on, "You get paid 4% of their recurring monthly bills. At an average of $60 per customer per month, your monthly commissions and overrides will be over $70,000 per MONTH – PLUS BONUSES."

Do people really do that?

"Yes," he went on, "that's why successful network marketers are some of the highest paid professionals in the world. They have built teams that have put a lot of business on the books."

If an average person can learn the skills and build a money machine like that, can you see why I'm excited about network marketing?

What if you could do just 25% that well? Would an extra $18,000 a month in residual income change your life?

The Key to Duplication

1. Learn the simple skills
2. Gather a few customers
3. Find a few people who want to earn extra money
4. Pass it on
5. Teach them to pass it on

Can you do that? If you can, it will change your life *forever!*

Setting Goals in Your Business

There are 5 financial goals you need to work for in your business. Read this section over and then share it with your upline mentor. Every network marketing company is different. Your mentor will know what is realistic in your company.

1. Your First Paycheck

You want to earn your first paycheck as soon as possible. Many companies have a system in which you can earn some cash your first few days in the business. Sell something. Or buy something from yourself to get a fast paycheck. Make a copy of the paycheck when you get it and keep it.

2. The $300 Club

$300 a month is a magical amount in network marketing. It is the watershed where a new network marketer becomes convinced their network marketing career is working, and where they make the decision to redouble their efforts to go full time.

People who are consistently making $300 a month seldom quit. Often they redouble their efforts to get to $1,000 and beyond.

Try to get to $300 a month in consistent income within your first few months and then go from there to full time.

3. Job Optional (Full Time)

In many network marketing companies, a person can build their organization to the point where they are earning a full time income in 1-4 years. This means that your network marketing income is big enough to completely replace the income from your job. Remember, this income is different from your job income. This is residual income, so if you take 3 months off, you will still be getting paid.

4. Work Optional

This is network marketer's Heaven. Work optional means that you have enough residual income that you will never have to work again. Actually, at this point, you should continue working your business, but it can be at a much more relaxed pace. When I reached this point, I was able to work a few hours a month. You'll be the envy of your friends and family.

5. Your Dream Lifestyle

The last goal is where you have everything you want. Do you want a 10,000 square foot house at the beach? Do you want your own private plane? Do you want your own vacation house in Maui? Or maybe you want to build a school or finance a special missionary project. You can do it, because you are making that kind of money.

Setting Your Goals

Consult with your upline mentor and team leader to come up with realistic dates for reaching these goals and then write them in here.

My Financial Goals and Dates

1. First Paycheck..._____

2. $300 a month ...._____

3. Job Optional.._____

4. Work Optional ...._____

5. Dream Lifestyle Income ...._____

---

11 The 4 Gears of Network Marketing

Have you ever driven a stick shift (standard transmission) car? If you have, you know you shift into 1st gear to get started, but you very quickly shift into 2nd, then 3rd and finally, when you get up to speed, 4th gear.

You will go through 4 distinct stages of your business as you progress to the top in your business.

At first, it may seem that progress is slow. You won't get much out of get much out of the work you put in at first, but keep going. It will build.

Somebody asked a successful networker how much he made his first month in the business.

"I don't know," said the networker, "because I'm still getting paid, every month, for the work I did the first month. The total isn't in yet."

As people get up to speed, their incomes tend to multiply.

1st Gear – Your Warm Market

We cannot do great deeds unless we're willing to do
the small things that make up the sum of greatness.
-- President Theodore Roosevelt

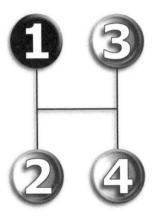

When you're in 1st Gear, you can't drive very fast, and you can't drive very far. What good is 1st Gear, then? It has a very important function. It gets you going! It takes you from 0 to 10 or 15 mph.

Your warm market consists of the people you know. It includes your friends, neighbors, family, co-workers, friends from your church and the people you do business with – your dry cleaner, hairdresser, pharmacist, etc.

Your warm market is important for several reasons:
1. That's where you get your practice.
2. Your warm market will help you reach your first goal – your first paycheck.
3. You might just change one of your friends' lives with a lucrative new career.

It's just like driving a car – you won't be in 1st Gear very long – just long enough to get going. That doesn't mean you won't be sharing with your warm market after that. It's just that your main focus will be elsewhere.

When you're driving, 1st gear gets you up to the speed where you can shift into 2nd Sharing with your warm market preps you to shift into 2nd Gear – your cold market.

Don't get into the warm market rut.

Many network marketers get very excited about the business and contact their warm markets quickly. Once they have finished with their warm markets, they don't know what to do next. (That's why you need a good upline mentor). Then they do one of 2 things:

1. Go back to their warm market - OR
2. Quit

Going back to the warm market

Your friends will listen to you the first time you approach them. Some might listen a second time. If you keep going back to them, however, you will end up in the NFL Club (No Friends Left). You don't want that. Your friends – and your business – are too important for that.

Doing the Unthinkable

Other network marketers figure they have reached all the people they know, so it didn't work for them. Then they quit.

Quitting is not an option. You joined the business to make money and change your life. If you quit at this point, you haven't begun to learn how to be successful in the business yet.

What if your child took a few steps when she was learning to walk – then fell down – and quit trying to walk? What if your child spent the rest of her life crawling around on her hands and knees because she decided that learning to walk was just too hard? What a tragedy that would be. What a tragedy it is that so many people quit when the going got rough – before they were able to realize their potential in their network marketing business.

1st Gear activities

1. Learn the basics of your product
2. Familiarize yourself with your website and your company's website. Learn the back office.
3. Learn a script for sharing and recruiting.
4. Make your Top 40 List
5. Get started in your upline's training system
6. Earn a paycheck your first month
7. If your company has a fast start bonus, go for it!

2nd Gear- Your Cold Market

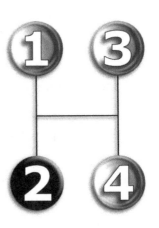

You got the momentum started in 1st Gear. Great! Use that momentum to shift into 2nd Gear.

2nd Gear is where you learn to attract and approach people you don't know. These people are called your cold market. There are many ways you can find cold market people to talk to. Some of them include:

1. Meet people when you are out. Get their contact information and get back with them within 48 hours.
2. Go to Chamber of Commerce functions, such as mixers and breakfast or lunch meetings. (I am a member of 4 chambers of commerce in my local area).
3. Join a networking group.
4. Buy a table or booth in a business expo or career fair.

5. Run newspaper ads (Be careful, you can spend a lot of money on ads, and cheap ads are usually not effective. That's why they're cheap).
6. Attract people to your web site and give you their email address for more information.
7. Purchase network marketing leads.

2nd Gear is where you get the paychecks coming in regularly. It's important to keep the momentum going to and continually build on it.

The time will come, when you're in 1st or 2nd Gear, that you won't need your upline mentor to continue making 3-way calls. You will be able to make the calls and presentations by yourself. Soon you will be the upline mentor to your people, and you will be making 3-way calls with your own downline. The genius of network marketing is that each generation of distributors "grows up" and trains the next generation.

In 2nd Gear you are developing a downline. It is essential that you begin to function as a leader for your team in 2nd Gear. Learn leadership skills. Read books and listen to recordings on leadership. I recommend anything by John Maxwell on leadership.

I listen to several books a month. I am constantly updating my list of recommended listening and reading on the web site. Check the Resource section of my web site, www.ITrainMillionaires.com to select and order the materials that will help you grow. In network marketing, you must grow if you want your business to grow.

When driving a car, 2nd Gear might take you from 10 mph to about 25. In network marketing, 2nd Gear can develop a residual income sufficient to cover a car payment every month. It can also set you up for more good things within a few months. You're not full time yet, but you're getting there.

3rd Gear – Building and Leading Your Team

A leader is one who knows the way,
goes the way and shows the way.
-- John C. Maxwell

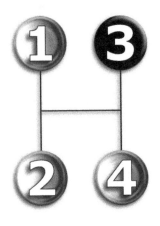

As you build your downline you will be developing leadership skills. Just as your upline took responsibility to encourage you and help you get into the habit of getting trained and working your business, you will be taking more and more responsibility for your new team members.

Of course the goal is to get them to take over most of that responsibility for themselves as quickly as possible, but you need to help them grow to that point.

The time will come in 3rd Gear that you will be able to go full time in the business. This is where the fun really starts, because your income is no longer dependent on the number of hours you work per week. Your income is determined by the value you bring to your team and to your company through your team's efforts.

If you really love your job, you don't have to go full time, but you can do it any time you want. It's called being Job Optional, and it's a great feeling not to need your job any more. When you go full time, you will have more hours to build your business and make even more money.

Many successful network marketers never get to 4th Gear, but enjoy 6-figure residual incomes in 3rd Gear.

While in 3rd Gear, enjoy your success. Take 2-3 vacations per year. But when you get back from vacation, go back to work. The best is yet to come – when you're in 4th Gear.

4th Gear – Developing Leaders

I think what separates a superstar from the average ballplayer is that he concentrates just a little bit longer.
-- Hank Aaron, Baseball Star

3rd Gear is where you become an effective leader for your team. 4th Gear is where you develop downline leaders who no longer need to depend on you for leadership and support.

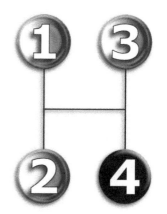

4th Gear leaders often earn $300,000 to over $1,000,000 per year in residual income, and this income continues to go up because of the efforts of their downline leaders and their teams.

Will you still work hard in your business? That's your choice. You can, but you don't have to at this point. Many 4th Gear leaders have learned to love the business so much that they continue building and growing.

4th Gear network marketers enjoy some of the highest incomes in the country – on par with CEO's of some very large corporations. The difference is, they rose to their income level much easier, and they have much more time to enjoy their income because it is residual.

12 How to Invite Your Friends to Join Your Business

The people you know are sometimes called your *warm market*. These are the people who will talk to you when you call them because they know you. Although they are the easiest people for you to talk to, they can be the most difficult people to present your business to, but they shouldn't be.

> **The first thing you need to recognize is this: If you are in a good business, then network marketing isn't something you do *TO* people, it's something you do *FOR* people.**

If you've found something good, why wouldn't you want to share it with a friend? After all, if you've seen a good movie, discovered a good restaurant or found an inexpensive place to get your car repaired, wouldn't you tell a friend? Of course you would. If you've found a great way to make abundant residual income to change your life, why wouldn't you want your friends to have it too?

Sometimes people say, "I don't want to make money off my friends." If you worked for a carpet company and your friends needed a new carpet, would you want them to come to you, or to go to a stranger? Don't you think your friends would rather give you the business than give it to a stranger? The same is true for your network marketing business – especially if you are marketing a Quadrant 1 product – something they know they need and are already using.

"Whyyyy Didn't You Tell Me?"

When I joined my former company a number of years ago, I contacted a lot of my friends, but not all of them. I didn't think some of them would be interested. Big mistake!

About 9 months later, one of my friends called me to tell me about a great network marketing business he had just joined. As he began to explain it, I recognized he was talking about my company – the same business I didn't think he'd be interested in!

"Dennis," I said, "I joined the company several months ago, and I've made thousands of dollars in it."

"Whyyyyy didn't you tell me?" he asked. "I'd much rather have joined under you!"

I can't tell you how bad we both felt. To make matters worse, nobody in his upline offered anything to help him prosper in his business. Worse yet, his sponsor would not even return his calls. Dennis floundered and failed. Had I shared the business with him, he would have had all the help I got. He would have had a much better chance of succeeding, and we both would have benefitted. Had I shared the business with him, it would have strengthened our friendship too.

Don't Prejudge People.

I didn't call Dennis because I didn't think he would be interested in network marketing. He had never expressed any interest in business, and I didn't think he was the type to try. Wow! Was I ever wrong!

Don't prejudge people, or you'll miss some great opportunities to build your business. If they're really not interested, let them tell you.

Treat Your Friends as Friends, not Merely as Business Prospects

Your friends are your friends first, and potential business partners or customers second. You don't want to lose your friends over a business opportunity. You don't have to lose your friends if you handle it right.

How to Approach Your Friends

"I've found something that really good, and I immediately thought of you. You may or may not be interested, but I think you should know about it. Could we get together tomorrow?"

If they say, "What is it?" don't tell them yet.

You can answer by saying, "That's why we need to meet. I really need to show it to you. Would 7:00 be a good time?"

It is impossible to make an intelligent decision without adequate information

"I'm going to ask your opinion, and I know you need enough information to offer an intelligent opinion. Does that make sense to you"

Resist the temptation to tell them a little bit. Most of the time people make a decision on the little bit they hear, and then they are not open to hear the whole story. They make a decision before they have enough of the good information necessary to make an intelligent decision.

Approaching a Fiend You Haven't Talked to for a Long Time

It's easier today to connect with old friends than at any time in history. With Facebook, Twitter, LinkedIn, Classmates.com and other sites, it's easy to find a lot of the people you used to know. You can even Google their names and they might pop up. And don't forget your class reunions.

If you haven't talked to a friend for a long time, give them a call and catch up on the things that are going on in both of your lives.

Don't tell them about your network marketing business yet. Use the first call to reconnect.

If you share your business on the first call, you will probably lose them. They'll think you are not really interested in them, but in the money you can make from them.

Ask them about their family, the things they've been doing since you last talked with them. Ask them about their work. When they tell about their work, listen for signs of discontent, such as:

- They don't like their boss
- They're bored with work
- They aren't making enough money
- The commute is bad
- They're having trouble with co-workers
- Their job isn't very secure
- They don't like the hours
- The company is taking advantage of them

Take notes on any negative comments they make about their job. Don't grill them for comments, and don't comment on their negativities. Recent surveys have shown that as many as 80% of Americans are not happy with their jobs, so it is quite likely your friend is in that camp.

Wait a week or two after your initial call. Then call them again. After sharing some pleasantries, you can say something like this:

"You know, Sam, when we were talking the other day, you said something that really made me think about you. Do you remember when you said you are not happy with your boss, and that you're not making enough money?

"Well, I've been doing something recently that is solving those problems for me. I've been thinking I've got to share it with you – it might be just right for you, too."

(If they're local, continue with) "I don't have much time right now, but could we get together tomorrow?"

(If they are not local) "I really don't have much time to talk now, but could we set up a time to talk in the next day or two?"

Then, (local or not) follow up with: "Great. Let's pick a time that is good for both of us. Do you have your calendar handy?" (Always ask if they have their calendar handy. You want them to write the appointment down).

Set a time and date. If they ask what it's about, remind them you don't have much time right now, and that is why you wanted to set up a time when they would both have 15-20 minutes.

Don't Give Partial Presentations

If you don't have time to give a full presentation, make an appointment to do it later.

Incomplete presentations give incomplete information which is never adequate for a prospect to make an informed decision about your business. Many people will say no when they don't have enough information to get them to a yes.

You want them to get all the right information at one sitting so they can have a good picture of the business and make an informed decision.

What to Do When You Get Together

If you're new in the business

If your upline mentor is with you, edify them. "I'd like to introduce Sam, my business partner (or mentor – just don't say "upline"). Sam has been very successful, and he loves to help other people achieve their income potential, too."

Turn it over to Sam. When he begins presenting, listen attentively, nod your head. Don't say anything unless you are addressed. An occasional "yes," or "uh-huh" is OK, because it shows you are listening and you are in agreement with what he is saying. Do not interrupt his presentation.

If you are doing it alone, you can say something like this:

"I've got some friends who are making a lot of money in business. They are training me to do what they are doing, and they said it is OK for me to invite a couple of my friends too. I'd like to invite you to take a look and see if it is for you. "

What to do if your friend is not interested after the presentation

Leave the door open for another presentation in the future.

You can ask your friend to be your customer. Then ask, "After a few months and my business is growing, is it OK if I get back with you and let you know how I'm doing?"

How to Invite Your Friends to Join Your Business

Many times a friend won't join you until they see you are making money and the business is working for you. This leaves the door open for another more effective presentation that could motivate them to join.

Remember, your friendship is more important than the business you could be doing with your friends. After my initial approach to my friends, I always tell them something like this:

I hope you find value in what I'm doing, and I would really love to have you join me. However, I want you to know that your friendship is a lot more valuable to me than any business we could do. If you join me, great! If you don't, I want you to know that it will not change the way I feel about you as a friend.

13 How to Approach People about Your Business

Your prospects are everywhere. Have some business cards printed up. Make sure they look professional. They should include your phone number, your email address and your web site. Carry your business cards with you everywhere you go. You never know when you will meet an ideal prospect for your business and you will need to give them a business card.

I personally prefer to carry a card that does not have my company name or website on it. I have my own website that gets peoples' curiosity and invites them to give me their email address for more information. When they fill out the form on my web site, their information goes into my autoresponder – a system that automates my email follow up. When they ask for more information, here's what happens:

1. Their name and email address are added to my database.
2. They immediately get an automated email from me asking them to verify that they asked for the information, and that they give me permission to send them emails from time to time. (This is called *double opt in,* which assures them that I do not want to send them unwanted emails,

and it assures me that I can send them emails legally, subject to anti-spam laws.).

3. I get an email telling me that somebody asked for more information.
4. They receive an email from me with a special report on how they can make money from home.
5. They are redirected to a page with a video that gives more information.

There is a reason I do not like to mention my company on my business card. A lot of people have heard of my company, and a lot of them have a misconception of the power of our business opportunity. Maybe they know someone who tried our company at one time and failed. I don't want them to say no to the opportunity based on something they only think they know. If they say no, I at least want them to know what they are saying no to.

Once I have a chance to give them a presentation, I will tell them the name of my company. If they say they know the company, I ask, "Then you know about the simple skills that make people successful in our company, is that correct?."

When they say no (or ask what the skills are), I say, "If you don't know the simple skills and the system that makes people successful, you really don't know the most important things. Would it be OK if I fill you in on the important stuff?"

Approaching People about the Opportunity

You can start with a question, or with a statement and a question. Try several approaches and use the one that works the best for you. Whatever you do, you want to get their attention and pique their curiosity. You want to get their name, best phone number and best email address. You want them to be so curious and interested that they are dying to hear more.

How to Approach People About Your Business

Compliment the person first. Then open the conversation about your business.

The Waitress with a Million Dollar Attitude

Recently, while having lunch at a local restaurant, my wife and I were served by one of the best waitresses I have ever met in my life. She was really, really good. She came quickly with a big smile, a happy positive attitude, and a warm friendly greeting. She was attentive to us and our needs, and she made us feel important to be her customers.

I thought to myself, "What a waste. She's got a million bucks worth of people skills, and she's only making a few hundred dollars a week in the restaurant, because she doesn't know what she's really worth."

It was late in the afternoon on the 4th of July, and there were only two other customers in the restaurant, so we had a little time to talk. I asked her how long she had been working there.

"Six years," she replied.

"Then you must really love your job," I commented.

"Oh, yes, I really love working here."

I then asked her, "Would you be open to an opportunity to make a lot more money?"

"Oh, yes, I would," she answered.

"We help people like you find a way to multiply their incomes in their own businesses. Some of the people we've helped have developed 6-figure incomes. There is a small cost to get started, and most people qualify for a government program that effectively reimburses the costs of starting and running their businesses.

"You can start part-time without quitting your job. Even when you are making a whole lot more money than you're making here, you can still work here if you love it that much. You'll be in control of your life."

She gave me her phone number and address. When we were leaving, she said, "Please call me."

The Wal-Mart Cashier Who Wanted my Job

I was checking out at Wal-Mart. The cashier asked, "How's it going?"

"Super," I replied, "but it's getting better."

"Really?" said the cashier, "that sounds really good."

"Yeah, it is," I answered, "because I'm getting a pay raise every month."

"Really?" he said, "I wish I had your job."

Wow! He opened a door wide enough I could drive a truck through it!

"You're in luck," I responded. "We've got an opening right now, and I've been assigned to find someone to fill it. Give me your best phone number, and maybe we can talk tonight or tomorrow when you aren't working."

I got his number, met with him, and he joined my business.

There are many other ways to open a conversation about your business. Your upline mentor may have some approaches that work particularly well for your company, so be sure to discuss this with him or her.

How to Introduce Yourself to a Stranger

Whatever you do, be friendly, be polite, be positive, smile, and look people in the eye. Reach out to shake their hand as you introduce yourself. You want them to like you from the start.

How to Approach People About Your Business

You want to introduce them to your business, but what you really want is for them to ask you what you do for a living. Here's how to get them to ask you. It works almost every time: It works so well, that in the thousands of times I've tried it, there have only been a handful of times the other person didn't ask me what I do.

Once you have introduced yourself, ask them what they do for a living. It's simple.

"Tom, it's really good to meet you. What do you do?" (In the US, everybody understands that you are asking them what they do for a living).

When they ask you what you do, don't tell them about your job. Don't tell them that you are a network marketer for XYZ Company. Give them a benefit statement – a statement that explains the benefit they will receive from knowing you and joining your business.

This type of introduction is sometimes known as your elevator speech. Think of meeting someone in an elevator. You have 20-30 seconds to make the connection or you will lose the opportunity forever. You want to say something that will spark an interest so you can get their phone number.

Here are some samples:

If you're starting haven't made much money yet

Use your upline mentor or someone in your upline who is very successful: Borrow their story or testimony until you have your own.

"I work with an income mentor who trains people to double or triple their incomes, and I'm looking for people who are interested in taking a look."

"I work with a very successful businesswoman who teaches other people how to have their own businesses and live their dreams, and I'm looking for people who are interested."

You could follow up with: "Is that something you might be interested in?"

You are fishing to see if they will bite. If they do, get their name, their best phone number and their best email address. (Most people have more than one. You want the phone they answer and the email address they check daily).

You could also follow up with: "We have some openings for people to start part-time while they keep their regular jobs. Is that something you might be interested in?"

Get their contact information if you can. Then schedule a meeting or a call. Use your upline mentor if you are new in the business.

If you are making about $1,000 or more per month in residual income:

"I work with an income mentor. I help people develop their own businesses so they can have the lifestyle they've always wanted. I'm looking for people who are interested in upgrading their lifestyles."

"I teach people how to have their own businesses, multiply their incomes and live their dreams. Is that something you might be interested in?"

If they express interest, get their contact information and make an appointment for a time when they would have 20-30 minutes so you can fill them in on the details. Always ask for the best phone number to reach them and the best time to call.

Your Follow-Up Call

"Hi, Joan, this is Bob. We met the other day at Starbucks. I'd like to set up a time to get together so I can fill you in on the details of what we were talking about then. Would this evening work for you, or would tomorrow evening be better?"

It's always good to give them a choice of times. It makes it easier for them to say yes when you don't give them the option to say no.

Always use the words "to fill you in on the details" as the purpose of the appointment. It is non-threatening and void of any pressure.

Although, as a general rule, I do not like using pressure in dealing with people, there are times I feel it can be appropriate:

1. When a person has said no without knowing the facts, I sometimes try to "push" them a little bit to get the right information so they can make an informed decision. An uninformed "no" is a bad decision, especially since they are deciding against something that could change their life.

2. Some people are natural fence-sitters. They have a hard time making any decision without a little push. When I

sense I am dealing with this type of person, I try to give them that little push.

You want to make people feel comfortable with you and your business. You want to present everything in such a way that people will be eager to join, to go to work and change their lives. I remember pushing a lady to join my previous business, and she made a lot of money.

Sell the Dream

When you were young, what were your dreams for your life? What did you want to do when grew up? You were full of dreams of the things you wanted to be and accomplish. When I was young I wanted to be a major league baseball player, then a DJ on the radio and a Grand Ole Opry star. I also wanted to be rich and not have to work.

Did any of that come true? I was a DJ for a few years, then I became a talk show host in Detroit. Many years later I got to the place where I didn't have to work – 4th Gear in network marketing.

Congratulations! You're Fired!

When I got to my dream lifestyle in network marketing, I tried to get my wife to quit her job, because I wanted to travel, and we didn't need the money. She wouldn't quit. We took 4 vacations that year. When we got home from the last one, there was a fax on our machine from her boss. It told her she was fired because she was traveling too much. I got her fired from her job!

I was the first one to see the fax. After reading it I exclaimed, "Congratulations! You're free! You just got fired!"

The real dream was not having to work. It didn't mean I didn't work. It's just that I didn't have to work. That dream was fulfilled by my career in network marketing. I got to that point a little over 3 years after starting in the company. We never bought the big house. We bought rental properties instead.

What is your dream? It probably has something to do with time and money, right? Time to spend with your family, time to do the things that are the most important to you. Time to travel, to do volunteer work, to do anything you want. The only way to have that kind of time is to have the money to support your family without working. Time, money and quality of lifestyle are all intertwined. Network marketing can give you the time and the money to live the life of your dreams.

When you go to your company's convention, get to know some of the people who are already enjoying that lifestyle – especially those in your own upline. Ask them what it's like, how long it took to get it and what they had to do to get there. Ask them what they sacrificed to achieve the lifestyle of their dreams.

Get a firm grip on your dream. Reach out for it by going the extra mile to develop your business and help your downline grow theirs. Talk about it to your downline. And talk about it to the people you are trying to recruit in the business.

Get sold on the dream yourself. Commit yourself to the dream. Then sell the dream. Read the motto below. I created it for my team, because I want everybody on my team to have it all – all the time and money to do what they want..

My dream is that I don't want to be spending all my working hours chasing dollars. There are things that are much more important in life, and I want to have lots of time to do them.

> **Some people have a lot of time but no money;**
> **It's because they don't work hard enough.**
> **Some people have a lot of money but no time;**
> **It's because they don't work smart enough.**
> **The most successful people have BOTH.**
> -Bob Sharpe

Posture Yourself

Some network marketers sound desperate for business. They act as if they really need people to join their downline. They sound needy. Nobody wants to join the downline of a needy person. People want to join an organization that knows how to be successful and is doing it. Successful people are not needy.

Realize that, when you recruit a new distributor and get them into your (or your team's) mentoring program, you are doing them a favor and helping them. Have that attitude when you share the business. You want them to join your downline, but you don't need them. You have a good thing going, and you are offering it to them. If they don't join, they miss everything. As for you, you are already on the way to reach out to your next prospect. You know that a certain number of the people you talk to will join and work the business.

Don't be arrogant when doing this. Arrogance turns people away. Be positive and confident. Confident leadership attracts the right kind of people, and that's what you are looking for – the right kind of people. You are on the road to your dream lifestyle, regardless of which of your prospects join you.

14 Keep Your Waiting Room Full

Your Top 40 List Is Your Waiting Room

Earlier in the book, we talked about making your Top 40 List. That is your list of at least 40 prospects you will talk to concerning the business. It can be more than 40, but it can't be less if you want to succeed. Always have at least 40 people on your active list at all times. If you don't have prospects, you can't build your business.

Your list is always changing. As you find new prospects, add them to the list. As existing prospects either join or turn down the offer to change their lives, take them off your Top 40 List, but keep them on your email list until they opt out or die. You always want your Top 40 List to be current, and you always must have at least 40 on it at all times.

When you go to the doctor, where do you go first? You go to the waiting room. This is where you and the other patients wait their turn to see the doctor.

Your Top 40 List is your waiting room. These are the people who are waiting their turn to be presented with the opportunity that can change their lives and make their dreams come true.

Some of the people in your waiting room might be excellent prospects, but the timing might not be good for them. They might be going through a particularly tough time at work. They could be preparing to go on vacation, or they could be going through a divorce. Others might be almost ready to join, but they're still doing their due diligence or trying to convince a reluctant spouse. That's OK. You'll eventually get some of them if you stay in contact with them.

For other people, the timing is now. A lot of people will be ready to start if someone shows them the reasons for starting now.

If you present to them and they are dragging their feet, you could ask them, "Is there any reason why you would want to start making more money later rather than sooner?"

If they say they are not ready yet, ask them, "What would it take to get you to the point where you are ready? Is there something I need to explain better?"

When you keep your waiting room full, you will always have people to talk to about your business, so keep your waiting room full.

Successful network marketers are skillful at finding people and adding them to their list – their waiting room. When you do that, it's as if you always have people standing in line to talk to you about your business.

Get them onto your list and then into your business as quickly as possible.

15 Where to Find Prospects to Recruit

 They're everywhere. 80% of Americans are unhappy with their jobs. A survey by USA Today a number of years ago revealed that 96% of all Americans had thoughts at one time in their lives that they would like to own their own businesses. Almost everybody needs to make more money. And a lot of people don't have much job security. In short, this country is chock full of people who want the benefits of what we have to offer. They just don't know how to get them.

Almost Everybody You Know Is a Prospect

Put them in your "waiting room" on your Top 40 List and share with them. You can tell them, "You may or may not be interested. That's OK. You're an intelligent person, and I believe you like to make intelligent decisions. I just want you to have enough of the right kind of information so that you can make an intelligent decision. Does that make sense to you?"

Most people consider themselves to be intelligent people, and most will say yes to that question, and when they do, they are opening the door for you to give them a presentation. Give it all you've got.

Almost Everybody You Meet Is a Prospect

Get their interest. Then get their contact information and follow up as soon as possible. When you are following up on a stranger, do it quickly, before they forget who you are.

You can wear a button or badge.

One network marketing company that specialized in weight loss products gave their distributors buttons to wear that said, "LOSE WEIGHT NOW ASK ME HOW." Those buttons get a lot of attention in a nation of overweight people where almost everybody wants to lose weight, but nobody wants to change their eating habits.

What kind of button could you wear that presents you as a person they need to know in order to better their lives? It could either promote your product or your business opportunity.

In my area, a lot of Realtors® wear professional engraved name badges when they are out in public. The badges simply give their name, the title Realtor® and the name of their company. You can order these badges at an office supply store.

What if you wore a professional engraved badge that had your name and underneath your name said something like this:

- Income Consultant
- Early Retirement Consultant
- Lifestyle Consultant
- Success Mentor

Enter the Room of Business

What if you could walk into a room full of successful businesspeople who were there to learn about you and your business? You can. It's your chamber of commerce. That's what the words chamber of commerce mean – room of business.

A chamber of commerce is not a government agency. It is a non-profit business organization that exists to promote local businesses and to foster a profitable business atmosphere in their area. Because they do a lot of good for their cities, some chambers get funding from their cities. They are there for one reason – to promote business. They will promote your business if you're a member.

Most chambers of commerce have at least 2 networking events every month. These events are specifically designed to be places where businesspeople can go and share. Of course, to earn a hearing, you have to listen to the other members tell about their businesses too.

How to Act in Chamber of Commerce Meetings

Most of the people in chamber of commerce meetings are successful in their fields of endeavor. Don't be intimidated if they are all more successful than you are. Be friendly and confident, and treat them like your peers. Don't look up to them, and of course, don't look down on them. They are just normal people, even if they are more successful than most.

Dress well. Here in Southern California, business casual works fine. In some other areas you might want to wear a business suit.

The Kinds of People You Will Meet in the Chamber of Commerce

For the most part, you will meet four kinds of people in the networking meetings:

1. You will meet local businesspeople.

They usually go because they have learned that it's good for business. They have learned that participation in the networking events helps them get new customers and maintain relationships with existing customers. Although they are looking for new customers, they are also open to meeting new people who want their business, also. Most of these people will be more open to your product or service than to your busienss opportunity, so lead with the product when you are talking to them.

2. Representatives of local businesspeople

Sometimes local businesspeople do not go, but they send an employee to represent them. These employees do not own their own businesses, and they can be open to either your product or your business opportunity. Lead with the product publicly. Get their business cards and call them within 48 hours to see if they are open to another income opportunity. Always call their cell phones and not their office phones to help them avoid an awkward situation. Also, get their personal email address, not their email address from their company for the same reason.

3. Salespeople

These are the independent reps and the reps for other companies who are trying to sell to the local businesspeople.

Many of these people do not own their own businesses, and very few of them have residual income. These can be some of your best prospects for recruiting. They are not afraid to talk to people, and many of them are very ambitious.

Again, it's normally not the best to speak about your opportunity in a chamber event, but to get their business cards and call them within 48 hours. Always call their cell phones and not their office phones.

4. Government officials

You may meet your city councilpeople, your mayor, and representatives of your state and federal legislators. I have found that most of these people are not good prospects for anything, but they are good to know if you ever have an issue with the government.

Your Commercial

At the breakfast and luncheon meetings, you will have a chance to stand up, introduce yourself and give a 60-second commercial about your business. Be prepared. Know what you are going to say ahead of time.

At a recent chamber of commerce breakfast meeting, two web designers got up and give their commercials.

The first one said,

> My name is ____, and I own _____, a local advertising company. I do web design, SEO and graphic design for brochures, business cards, post cards and other advertising work. If you need graphic design or a web site, please call us.

The second web designer said,

> You've got 9 seconds to live! (Pause) Not you, but your web site. A recent survey showed that visitors to your site have to see something that draws them in, in 9 seconds, or they will click away and be gone FOREVER. We know what to say and we know where to put it on your site so that won't happen to you. Also, a local chamber of commerce and a business in the area both LOST their web sites because of a simple mistake their webmasters made. When you become my customer, I'll tell you what it is so you won't ever have to lose your web site. My name is _____, and my company name is _____.

Which one of those web designers do you think got the most attention?

When you go to an event like this, have your commercial scripted. Don't focus on yourself and your business. Focus your commercial on problems your hearers may be facing and how you can offer the solution. If you do that one thing, your commercial will be more effective than 95% of the others you hear. Your hearers will be more interested, and they will remember you longer.

Here are some commercials used by network marketers. Which do you think are the most effective?

> I am with _____ Company. We have a full line of wonderful natural products to help you stay healthy and feel good. I am also looking for people to recruit into this wonderful business.

Have you ever wondered what people are saying behind your back? Look at her big butt. He sure is FAT! You've tried so hard to get rid of it, but food tastes so good – especially the junk. I've got the solution to zap your fat or your money back. Also, there are so many potential customers out there I can't possibly get them all myself. I've got openings for great people who want to earn a great income while they make a difference in other peoples' lives.

My name is _____. My company helps people save money on cell phones and other services. If you'd like to save money, please call me. I'm also looking for people to join my business. We earn residual income.

Are you paying too much for your cell phone? Yeah, I know you are, and you don't like it, either, do you? If you can give me 2 minutes, I can show you how to cut your monthly bill to ZERO – without sacrificing the quality you need. It could be the most profitable 2 minutes you've spent in a long time.

If you can think of a memorable tag line to end your commercial with, so much the better. A plumber in our local chamber of commerce always ends her commercial with, *"If it ain't flushing, we'll come a rushing."* She always gets a laugh, and nobody can forget her.

Practice your commercial over and over before you go. Do it in front of a mirror. Better yet, do it in front of a video camera and watch yourself perform. Make a cheat sheet – an outline of your commercial in a few words on the back of a business card, so you don't forget what to say. In the moments before your turn to speak, read over your cheat sheet outline several times. When you get up, hold the card in the palm of your hand and refer to it if necessary.

Write several commercials so you can change what you say from month to month and be fresh every time you go.

When you speak, smile, make eye contact with the people in the room, project your voice and speak with conviction and enthusiasm. A high energy commercial is always the most effective. Watch other people give theirs and learn from them.

I am a member of 4 chambers of commerce in my area, and I find my business relationships are very profitable. There are other perks, too. I also know many of the local movers and shakers and the local mayors, my state assemblyperson and my congressperson.

Several years ago, the California State Assembly was considering passing a bill that could put regulations on the dental plan my network marketing company was selling. (I am no longer with that company). I emailed my contact at the company and told him I knew the assemblyperson who was the chair of the committee that was considering the legislation. We knew each other because we had both been involved in the same chamber of commerce.

A few hours later I got a call from the CEO of our company asking me to call her and give her the company's position on the issue. He gave me an outline of what to tell her. I put in a call to her assistant. The next morning she called me back, and we spent almost a half hour discussing the bill. She thanked me for giving her a perspective that nobody in Sacramento had considered. That is another benefit of being involved in your local chamber of commerce. My connection helped our entire company, and it made me feel important. It's nice to feel important, isn't it?

Join a Networking Group

Networking groups are clubs that meet once a week for breakfast or lunch. They allow only one person from each business category to join and participate. A networking club, for instance, may have 1 dentist, 1 lawyer, 1 plumber, 1 chiropractor, 1 insurance agent, 1 florist, 1 banker, etc. They may have more than 1 network marketer, if the network marketers are selling different products. Most networking clubs have about 20-30 members.

Networking group meetings are somewhat similar to chamber of commerce breakfasts or luncheons, with a few differences. They focus on getting leads for their members, and they expect you to bring leads for other members regularly.

You will have the opportunity to get up and give your 60-second commercial. During your commercial, you will tell your fellow members the types of people or businesses that are the best leads for you, in the hopes that the other members will know and refer them to you. Of course, you are obligated to share leads with the others also.

Members of these networking groups usually form a close bond with one another in a spirit of mutual friendship and help.

While there are a few national and international organizations that have local networking chapters, there are also a lot of independent local networking groups.

The major networking groups are BNI, LeTip, Leads Club and TEAM Referral Network.

You can find more information in the Resources section of www.ITrainMillionaires.com .

After you have experience in a networking group, you might want to start your own. It's a lot of work and a lot of responsibility, but it can generate a lot of leads.

Use Sizzle Cards and Hot Pockets

Sizzle cards are business cards with a "sizzle message" to get people to contact you for more information.

You can buy them in large quantities and leave them wherever you go – gas pumps, store counters, public restrooms, restaurants (leave one with your tip), and other public places.

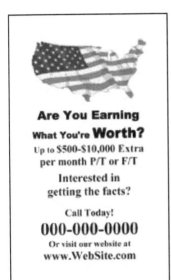

Are You Earning

What You're Worth?

Up to $500-$10,000 Extra
per month P/T or F/T

Interested in
getting the facts?

Call Today!

000-000-0000

Or visit our website at
www.WebSite.com

It's best to have a toll-free number where a person can call, hear a 30-second sizzle message and leave a message for you to call them back. You can find a good place for an inexpensive toll free number on our web site. Check the Resource Page at www.ITrainMillionaires.com for toll free numbers.

Hot Pockets are small clear poly envelopes with a slit on one side and removable adhesive on the back. Some people call them poly bags, but they're really not bags. They are made so you can slip some sizzle cards in the slit so they stick out and people can take them easily. They are very inexpensive, so you can stick them on gas pumps, bulletin boards, ATM machines, vending machines and other public places with high traffic. If the sizzle cards attract attention, people will see them and take one.

Put about 5-6 sizzle cards in the hot pocket and stick it up. One of my downline team members put hot pockets in a number of places on the way to work every morning, and he has recruited a number of people from them.

You can find more information in the Resources section of www.ITrainMillionaires.com,.

Use Social Media

Do you use Facebook? If not, create a Facebook account and learn to use it. Invite the people you know to be your friends on Facebook. Soon, some of their Facebook friends can become your Facebook friends too.

As you build your Facebook audience, you can build a fan page – a page that features your business. Your Facebook Profile is the page about you. Your Fan Page is the page to promote your business.

Also, get a Twitter account and learn to get your message out by "Tweeting." Follow others on Twitter, and others will follow you. The bigger your following, the more people you can potentially recruit.

Buy Leads

There are a number of companies that advertise on the Internet and elsewhere to generate leads of people who are interested in having a home based business. They then sell those leads to network marketers.

Some of the leads are very good; others are worthless. Whenever you buy leads from a company, buy a small quantity to start. That's enough to get a good feel for the quality of the leads.

One lead I got one time was a lawyer who was the mayor of a classy suburb of a large city. He was getting tired of the legal profession, and he was exploring his options.

Leads can cost as little as 5¢ each, or as much as $5.00 each. The nickel leads are usually not very good. The more expensive leads can be very good.

The best leads are called real time leads. When you purchase this type of lead, you will be notified immediately by email whenever a person fills out the form requesting more information. These are some of the best leads you can buy.

One time I got an email about a person who had just signed up for information. I called her immediately and shocked her. She was still looking at the web site when I called. She was so impressed; she listened intently to my presentation and joined my business.

Phone Surveyed Leads

Some lead companies offer leads where they have actually surveyed a prospect on the phone. Since the person has already been surveyed on the phone, they are expecting a call. You will know some things about them before you call. These leads can be very good, but they're also expensive.

Exclusive and Non-Exclusive Leads

Most of the leads you buy are not exclusive. They are sold to 2-4 different network marketers at the same time. When this is done, the lead companies are careful to not sell the same lead to more than one distributor from any one company. Non-exclusive leads, of course, are cheaper to buy. Most network marketers are not good presenters, so if you call your lead as soon as you get it, and if you make a good presentation, you will probably stand out from the others who call. Also, as crazy as it may seem, a surprising number of network marketers buy leads and never call them.

Long Form Leads

Some of the web sites that capture leads require the people to fill out a long form, asking for phone number, address, age group, why they're interested in a home business, etc. Leads with this much information are better, and they're more expensive. Most people won't give that much information. Those who do will tend to be better prospects. Also, they're easier to talk to, since you already have a lot of information about them.

Short Form Leads

These leads often give you just their name, email address and phone number. Since most people will only give this much information when asked for info, there are a lot more of these available, and they're cheaper. Most leads are short form leads.

Short form leads can be very good leads. Most of the leads my team and I have purchased are short form leads, and we've recruited a lot of people from them.

Aged Leads

The newer the lead, the better it is. Some companies sell old leads very cheaply. Aged leads are generally 30-90 days old. That means 30-90 days have passed since the people asked for information online, and the leads have been sold 4 or more times to other network marketers before they are sold as aged leads. These leads are never as good as fresh leads, but they can still be good.

16 Making Your Presentation

Every company has a presentation to train their distributors with, so we won't go into that here. However, there are a few things to know about giving your presentation.

Print out the PowerPoint Presentation they Give You

Insert the pages into sheet protectors and put it in one of the sections in your loose leaf binder.

Be Confident

Confidence is power. You are presenting a great opportunity that can change your prospect's life. Talk that way. Act that way.

Ask Questions and Listen

Be interested in your prospect. Listen to them. Don't just be thinking about the next thing you are going to say. People like it when you listen to them. You are showing them respect and that you are interested in them as people and not just as prospects for your business.

Realize You Are Helping People Get What They Want

Do you believe that most people would love to have the lifestyle where they had enough money coming in, automatically, so they wouldn't have to work? Of course they would. Some would continue to work. Others would quit their jobs to do volunteer work. And still others would quit all kinds of work forever. Almost everybody would love to have that option.

That is exactly what network marketing has to offer, and those of us who have found the key get to enjoy it. Almost everybody you meet would love to have it. Most of them want it badly enough that they would work for it if they believed they could have it. The disconnect is that most people believe it is out of their reach.

Your job is to help people believe the lifestyle of time and money is within their reach in a few years, and that you and your company can help them achieve it.

Remember, network marketing isn't something you do TO people, it is something you do FOR people.

If They Are Hesitant When You Close

Always assume they want to get started right away. If you have that assumption, your body language, your tone of voice and your choice of words will show it. You will make your prospect feel more comfortable saying yes.

"Do you have any questions before we get you started?"

OR

"Do you have any questions before you get started?"

17 Finding Prospects on the Internet

There are basically two ways to find prospects on the Internet:

1. Buy Leads
2. Generate Your Own Leads

There are advantages to both. Buying leads is the fastest way to have a steady stream of prospects, but there is a cost involved. As long as the profit from buying leads far outweighs the cost, I don't mind paying for them.

The advantage of buying leads is that, whenever you run out, you can always buy more at any time. When you generate your own leads online, you may or may not always have all the leads you need.

Generating your own leads takes time and skill, and it can also cost money. Many network marketers would rather buy the leads and spend their time and expertise in recruiting them.

The next chapter explains the different types of leads available for purchase. These leads are people who are looking for a home based business. You recruit them by calling them on the phone. You can build a downline nationwide with leads. This is one of the reasons you need unlimited long distance. In my previous network marketing company was not allowed to sell in a few States. I had downline in every State they operated in because of the leads my team and I bought and recruited.

Generating Your Own Leads

There are several ways of generating your own leads online.

Your Own "Squeeze Page" Web Site

It is important to have your own web site – other than the web site you get from your company – to generate leads for recruiting. Your company web site will be more geared toward giving people information. You need a web site that arouses interest and curiosity and motivates people to ask for more information.

All you need for this is a one-page site. This type of site is sometimes called a landing page, or squeeze page. An effective squeeze page gives people just enough information to cause them to ask for more.

A good squeeze page gets people's attention with a great headline. When people visit your site, you only have 9 seconds to get them interested, or they'll click away, so your headline is vital.

Follow it up with a paragraph or two, and maybe a few bullet points. Web surfers normally don't read long text unless they're looking for detailed information, so keep it short and to the point.

You might include a short video – 20 seconds to 1 minute. If your video is exceptional, you might get away with 2 minutes, but nothing longer.

The page should contain no other information, and it should have no links to click on. Instead, there is a form for them to give you their name, email address and phone number.

Everything on the page should drive them to give you their information on the form.

There should be a short disclaimer in smaller type promising people that you will not give their email address to anyone, and that you will not spam them.

When people fill out the form on the squeeze page, their contact information should go into an autoresponder. The autoresponder automates data collection and follow up.

Internet Prospecting System

An Internet prospecting system combines all the elements you need for lead generation, follow up and contact management into one system. I have been using one that has built in videos and a back office that features Internet training for network marketers. They even have regular training webinars. You can see more information in the Resources section of

www.ITrainMillionaires.com

Get a Domain Name

A domain name is the dot-com name a person enters online when they are looking for a web site. www.google.com is a domain name. The domain name is the address of the web site. It is sometimes called a URL (Universal Resource Locator).

Good domain names are hard to get. Most of the good ones are taken. Early on, some investors bought up a lot of good domain names so they could resell them at a profit. Some of the best domain names have resold for millions of dollars. I own a lot of very good domain names. I have spent hours thinking up possible names and checking online to see if they were available.

To find if your chosen domain name is available and to order it, you can get help on the Resources section of www.ITrainMillionaires.com for a form that will help you check if your chosen domain name is available. When you use it, it will take you to a place where you can get the best price on your domain name. (Most places sell them for less than $15 a year).

What to look for in a domain name

1. It should be a dot-com, not a dot-net or dot-something else.

Dot-com is the gold standard of domain names. When people look for a web site, they often type the .com by force of habit, even when they are looking for a .net web site.

2. It should be descriptive of a benefit you offer.

One of my web sites, www.ITrainMillionaires.com lets people know what to expect when they come to my site just by looking at the domain name. Yes, I really do train millionaires..

I used to own www.PaidForLife.com. I sold it several years ago.

3. It should be easy to spell and use common spellings of words whenever possible.

4. If there are variations of the spelling, you should register all variations.

If you get www.MoneyForMe.com you should also try to get www.Money4Me.com.

5. It should be as short as possible.

Easier said than done. Most of the short domain names are taken, just avoid something like:

www.ThisDomainNameIsWayTooLongDontYouThink.com

6. Get your own name, too, if you can.

While you're at it, check to see if your name is available as a domain name. I own www.BobSharpe.com and also www.BobSharpe.net. I still don't know what I'm going to do with the dot-net version of my name yet, but, since it's my name, I wanted it.

Domain names are not case-sensitive. Most people give out their domain names in all lower-case letters. If you capitalize each word in the domain name when you give it out, it will be easier for people to read and remember.

Getting People to Look at Your Web Site

In the Internet world, we call that driving traffic to your site. The best site in the world is useless if people don't see it. Once you get your site, it is your job to drive traffic to it. There are several ways to do this.

Offline ways to drive traffic to your site

1. Put your web site on your business cards.
2. Put it on every flyer and advertising piece you have.
3. Put it on your sizzle cards, along with your phone number.
4. Give it out wherever you can.

Driving traffic online

1. Organic search (free)

This is through finding you in your free listing on Google, Yahoo, Bing or other search engines.

There could be millions of web sites competing for the first page of Google under the key words home based business. Most people don't go past the first page when they are looking. If you are not on the first three pages, your chances of being found are very slim.

In order to get near the top with your free listing, you have to either be in a category where there are not many web sites, i.e., home businesses in Port Sanilac, Michigan, or you have to have your web site fine tuned to rise to the top through Search Engine Optimization.

How to do SEO is beyond the scope of this book. You can learn to do it yourself, or you can pay an SEO company to do it for you. The best SEO services can cost thousands of dollars per month to help you get the "free" advertising online.

2. Press Releases (free or paid)

There are sites where you can post press releases online. Write the release and post it with a link to your web site. The press release will help you in two ways: 1) people reading the press release will find a link to your site, and 2) the incoming link to your site will cause the search engines to move your site up in the rankings. Be sure that the press release you write is newsworthy, and not just an advertising message.

Write Articles (free or paid)

If you write one or more articles about the subject of your web site, there are a number of places online where you can post them. Just like the press releases, they will drive traffic to your site. A good article should have good keywords. It should be 95% information and no more than 5% advertising.

Social Media (free)

Do you have a Facebook account? When you write your profile for your account, write the stuff that will attract prospective network marketers to you. Your profile is your personal and career information. You can have only one profile page. You can have multiple Fan Pages.

Your fan page is your free Facebook business page. Create a fan page for your network marketing business. Ask people to go to your page and "Like" it.

You should also consider getting and using a Twitter account. Who would you like to have following you? Follow them, and many of them will reciprocate and follow you.

Video (free)

Create a YouTube channel and do a series of videos on the benefits of being in your business. Make them short and to the point. All of your videos should prominently display the URL of your squeeze page.

Use key words in the copy on your channel page and in the video file names.

You don't have to appear professional in your video. You are not David Letterman or Connie Chung, and people don't expect you to be as polished as them. Speak with conviction and enthusiasm. You have to be interesting and genuine.

Pay-Per-Click Advertising (paid)

When you search on Google, have you noticed that there are two or three listings on the top and along the right margin that are set off from the other listings? These are called sponsored ads. People pay for them.

Whenever anyone clicks on one of those listings, the advertiser is charged anywhere from a few cents to $25 or more. Paying for the click does not guarantee the person will become a customer. You are just paying to get them to your web site.

When using this method, you can bid the amount you are willing to pay per click. If you are outbid by the competition, your ad will show up very little, if at all.

You can set a budget when you order pay-per-click advertising. For instance, if you find that the going rate is 75¢ per click, you might bid 80¢.

You can set a budget. If your budget is $50 a month, you can tell Google, and the ads will stop once you have reached $50. You can also set a daily limit. Without it, you could use all your advertising dollars the first day of the month. Then you would have no ad exposure until the beginning of the following month. You could set a maximum of $3 a day. That way your advertising will be spread out through most or all of the month.

Checking the best key words and doing Pay Per Click advertising is a skill you can learn and develop. Unskilled people have lost money. Skilled people have made a fortune with it.

Facebook Advertising

Some people have found Facebook advertising to be very effective. Check out the advertising page on Facebook for details.

18 How to Recruit People on the Internet

You will never run out of people to talk to if you have a good source of leads. It's like having people standing in line to hear about your business. Many of my friends and downline partners practically built their businesses on leads they purchased. Some of the best network marketers I know started out as leads that their sponsors purchased from a lead company.

Most of the leads you get will never join you in the business. That is why you want to sort through the leads quickly to find the ones who are. It's like sorting through a deck of cards to find the Aces. If your company furnishes you with free leads, you have a big advantage – especially of the leads are highly targeted.

Don't buy leads, however, until you are in 2nd Gear in your business. Cut your teeth on your warm market. Get a few people in your downline first, so you have experience in recruiting and in selling your products or services.

When you purchase Internet leads, what do you do with them? Send them an email and hope they join? It almost always takes more than that.

Understanding What You Are Getting

The leads you purchase are people who have filled out a form online to receive information about having a home business. They are very generic, and the people have no idea about the details of the business.

While some of the people are very serious about building a thriving home business, many others are just curious. When you buy leads, you will get both kinds. You have to sift through the curious to find the serious people.

While you never know what you're going to get, if you purchase 100 leads from a reputable company, and if you do a good job of contacting them and following up, you will probably get 2-5 or more new people to join your organization.

Any way you cut it, it's a numbers game, and you have to go through the numbers to succeed. When you do, the success will be sweeter than you ever imagined.

Also, since most of the leads you will buy are shared leads, there will be other network marketers getting them the same time you do. The race is on. Be the first to call and build a relationship with the prospect, and you'll have a good chance of being the one he or she chooses to join.

Tools to Help You Present to Leads

Autoresponder

When you purchase leads from a legitimate lead company, you have permission to send them emails about your business, and you can put them in your autoresponder.

A good autoresponder will immediately send them a pre-written personalized email ("Dear George" not "Dear Friend") telling them you received their request about making money from home, and that you will be calling them shortly.

It will then automatically begin sending them a series of personalized follow up emails from you at intervals you determine.

For more autoresponder information, visit the Resource Section of www.ITrainMillionaires.com.

Sizzle Line

If you have a sizzle line, it will save time on your calls to leads. You can have them listen to part of the presentation on the sizzle line instead of having to give it to them. Your company should furnish this for you. You can be calling another lead while the first lead is listening to the presentation. Then you can call the first lead back later – preferably the same day, but not longer than 24 hours..

This does two things for you:

1. It gives a great presentation every time, assuming the sizzle line is good
2. It allows you to contact more people in less time

If you talk to a prospect and send them to the sizzle line, be sure to set the time to call them back. That gives them a sense of urgency to listen to the sizzle right now.

Ask your upline mentor if your company or your team has a sizzle line available for you to use with your prospects.

Skype

This is a free service you can get from www.Skype.com. If your computer has a webcam and microphone, you can talk face-to-face to anyone in the world who has Skype. When we were in China, we used it to talk to my children back in California. It worked really well, and it was free.

Web Conferencing Service

Web conferencing is an easy way to give a live presentation online to one or more people. A good web conferencing program will allow you to upload videos and PowerPoint presentations. Then when you are giving a presentation to a person online, you can start a video or PowerPoint with one click of the mouse.

We have a service available that you can use to present to 50 people at a time for less than $10.00 a month. Comparable services such as GoToMeeting and WebEx cost about $100 a month, and they lack some of the features the $10 program has. Find it on the Resource Section of www.ITrainMillionaires.com.

Use a Script

When you contact a lead by phone, it is extremely important that you use a script so you know exactly what to say to your prospect. Your script should be long enough to give the prospect enough information and the motivation to make an intelligent decision to join your business.

Ask your upline mentor for a script to use for calling leads. If they don't have one, try to find someone in your upline with a script they use that is effective in closing leads. An email to your team leader should do it.

Asking Questions

Part of your script will include the informal asking of questions to help you set the prospect at ease, to get to know them, and to probe to see what their "hot buttons" are. Ask friendly questions, but don't interrogate or ask anything too personal.

The person who asks the questions controls the conversiation. You must remain in control if you are going to accomplish anything in your presentation.

When you begin your presentation, tell your prospect, "You'll probably have questions for me. Please write them down, and when I finish explaining our business, I'll answer them. OK?"

If they try to ask a question while you are presenting, please remind them that you will take time to answer all their questions once you're through. The only exception to this is if they need you to repeat or clarify something you said while presenting.

When they ask questions, compliment them with "That's a good question." Then proceed to answer.

Then you can ask, "Do you have any other questions before you get started?"

If they ask a question you can't answer

If you don't know the answer to a question they ask, that gives you a great opportunity for a follow-up call if they don't join on this call.

"That's really a great question. Nobody has ever asked me that one before, and I'm afraid I don't have a good answer. Let me research that and get back with you, OK?"

Then you can ask, "Do you have any other questions before you get started?" Continue as if you had been able to answer the question. The unanswered question may or may not be enough to prevent them from joining on this call. If they don't join, you have a great reason to call them back and invite them into your business again.

The Close

The close is the call to action. It is what you do to close the "sale," to get people to join you in your business. This is the critical moment when your prospect could begin the journey that can change her life forever.

You already know she would like to better her life with the money and time freedom your networking marketing business can give her. Since you already know that, you should move forward with the assmumption that she will join you in your business.

After making a presentation, give a call to action. Your goal is for her to join on the spot. It's nice when that happens. When it doesn't, you want to move her one step closer toward joining so you can call her again.

Make it easy for your prospects to say yes

I never ask a person if they would like to join. That makes it too easy for them to say no. I've learned that a lot of people say no even when they would like to say yes, because they have an overly cautious or negative mindset, and it's just easier to say no.

One way you can close a prospect

1. Does that make sense to you?
2. How would you like your name printed on your paycheck?
3. What is the address to send the paychecks to?
4. What credit card would you like to put this on?

If they give you the information, it's an automatic YES. If they don't want to join just yet, they'll tell you.

If you are uncomfortable asking these questions, do it anyway. If you waver, or if you don't sound confident at this point, your prospect will be more reluctant to join you. Remember, success lies outside of your comfort zone. You'll be surprised at how effective these questions are and how comfortable you'll become asking them. It is very rare that prospects are uncomfortable when you ask them. In all the times I've asked them over the years, I can't remember one time that the other person seemed uncomfortable when I asked them.

Another close you can use

Ask your prospect, "Do you have any questions before you get started?"

If they do, answer their question and then ask, "Do you have any more questions before you get started?"

Keep answering the questions until they say they have no more questions. Then you can say, "Good, all we need to do now is get the paperwork out of the way so we can get your training started. "How would you like your name printed on your paychecks?"

Then proceed to ask the questions to fill out their application form. Some network marketing companies allow you to fill out the online form for your prospect. Others require that the prospect fills it out herself. Be sure to follow your company's rules here.

If your company requires the prospect to do it, ask if they are online now. If so, walk them through the signup process. If they say they will do it later, tell them, "It's very important to do it while I'm on the phone with you. There are some things on the form that might not be clear to you, and I can walk you through it quickly and easily."

If they say they will sign up later and you believe them, they have just sold you! You can be 80% sure they will not do it. It is very important for you to do everything you can to get them to sign up while you are on the phone with them.

Practice Your Script

Read it aloud over and over. Practice it until it doesn't sound like you are reading it. You don't want people to think you are reading a script when you call them.

If you want to introduce the business to your best friend, here's your chance. Practice it several times first. Then ask him or her to listen and critique your performance.

The Importance of Having a Good System

If you have a good system to follow, you can recruit 5 or 10 times more people than you could recruit without a system. Successful network marketers have great systems that are easy to follow and easy to teach to their new people.

1. A good system is proven to work for thousands of network marketers.

2. It makes the process of building your business simple.

3. It gives you a track to run on, so you always know what to do.

4. It gives you the power tools to get the job done effectively. (Like any other tools, however, they won't do a thing if you aren't using them).

5. Your prospects see the simplicity of the process you are following to recruit them. This gives them the confidence they can make money in your company, even before they join.

6. When people join, a system makes it easy to train them.

7. It's easier to have confidence and keep motivated when you know exactly what to do and how to do it. You get this from the system.

8. With the right system, you always have people standing in line to learn about your business. This is huge.

The Power Recruiting System

The Power Recruiting System is a semi-automated system to build you business. I have seen people who use it a minimum of 5 hours per week begin to build a great part-time business and progress to full-time with a few more hours per week.

There are a few things that make it work:

1. Leads.

If your company offers free leads, get as many as you can and work them. If your company does not furnish leads, purchase them from a reputable lead company. For recommendations, see the Resources section of www.ITrainMillionaires.com.

2. The Recruiting Machine

The Recruiting Machine is what makes your presentation for you. It is a 15-30 minute video of your presentation online. Your upline or your company should provide this for you.

This is not your company web site or the web site your company provided for you. Those sites have too many options and too many ways for a person to get sidetracked or lost. Although these sites can be very good, they are not good for this purpose.

The Recruiting Machine site has one page and no links to click away from it. There is only one thing a person can do on that site – watch a powerful video presentation and see a list of bullet points giving them the reasons and benefits for joining.

The page should prominently display the message, *"Get back with the person who sent you here."*

3. You ... yes, You!

You are the important element in the process. Having the leads and the tools will not do the job for you. *You* do the job. Theleads and tools help you get a lot more done when you go to work in your business.

Nothing will heppen until you pick up the phone and call the lead. This is where you succeed or fail. It is so easy NOT to pick up the phone. If you want to succeed in the business, turn the TV off, tell your family you won't be available for an hour or two, and call your leads.

Make sure you have practiced the script enough that you don't sound like you're reading it. Engage in a little small talk to get them talking, but don't overdo it. A minute or twos is usually enough. It is very important to try to get them to like you.

Smile and Dial!

Be positive and friendly. Smile when you talk. People can hear a smile on the other end. Some telemarketing firms put a mirror over the phone to help their people remember to smile.

> Without calling your prospects,
> a terrible thing happens.
> Nothing.

A lot of network marketers are using the Power Recruiting Script with great results. If they can do it, you can do it. Do it.

Power Recruiting System

People are standing in line
to hear about your business
from your Internet leads.

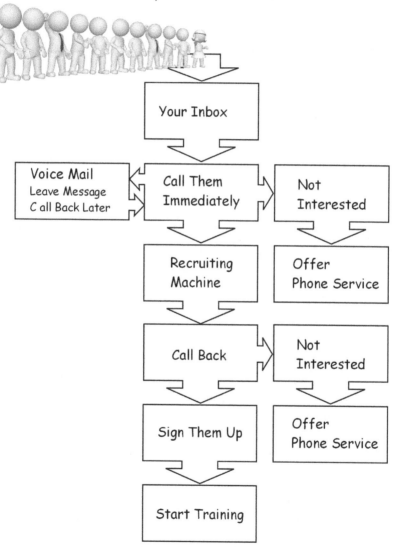

Your Inbox

Voice Mail Leave Message C all Back Later	Call Them Immediately	Not Interested
	Recruiting Machine	Offer Phone Service
	Call Back	Not Interested
	Sign Them Up	Offer Phone Service
	Start Training	

The Power Recruiting System Script

For this illustration, let's assume that I am calling a lady named Melissa in Nashville, Tennessee, and that I am working a network marketing company called ABC Company.

Hi, May I speak to Melissa, please?

(If another person answers the phone and asks why you are calling her, say, "I'm just calling to give her the information she requested online."

If they ask what kind of information, say, "It's about work, and I need to fill her in on the details.")

Hi, Melissa, My name is Bob Sharpe. I'm calling from Duarte, CA. We haven't met before, but you were on my web site recently looking for a way to make some money from home.

I'm calling to see if we are a good match for what you are looking for. Is that OK with you?

Great. I see you live in Nashville. That's one of my favorite cities. Have you always lived there?

We almost moved there a few years ago. In fact we even went house hunting in Brentwood. Then we decided to stay put, but I still love Nashville. (Any kind of nice small talik will do, but don't fabricate. We really did almost move to the Nashville area).

Melissa, what is it that caused you to go online to look for more income? (Let her talk)

What kind of work do you do?

Have you ever had a home business before? (If she answers yes, ask her what she did).

How to Recruit People on the Internet

Are you looking for extra income, or do you want to replace your current income? What is is it that you would like your home business to do for you? (Make note of her answer. This is what motivates her. Use it when you close her).

I don't know if we're a good match for you or not, but I'm going to give you a web site (or a phone number for a sizzle call) that will give you an overview of who we are and what we do. After going over it, you'll have a good idea if we are a good match for you. Does that make sense to you? (pause) Got a pen? (pause)

The web site is www.abccompany.com. (Spell it out clearly and have her spell it back to you).

When do you think you'll be able to look at it?

If you're interested, great. If you're not, that's OK too.

Should I call you back in an hour?

Good, I'm going to send you an email too, to your address melissa@melissa.com, so please watch for it. The subject line on the email will say *Our conversation today.* If you don't get it, please check your spam filter, OK?

Have a wonderful night (day). I'll talk to you in an hour

NOTE:

Your purpose on this call is not to give information, but to get people to the online presentation. If they ask for nformation, try to arouxe their curiosity. Tell them "That's what the web site is for. You need to see the visual part."

This call normally should not last more than 3-5 minutes, total.

Power Recruiting System Follow Up Call

Hi, Melissa, this is Bob Sharpe. How's everything in Nashville?

Did you get a chance to visit the web site?

(If she didn't, don't scold her. Make an excuse for her, so she'll feel comfortable with you. You can say, "Something always comes up, doesn't it? Would you be able to look at it right now for about a half hour?")

Melissa, what did you like best about what you saw? (Let her speak).

(If she is positive), Melissa, do you have any more questions before you get started? (Let her talk, and answer her questions).

If your company allows you to take their information and enter it yourself:

Melissa, how would you like your name printed on your paychecks? (Then asl all the other information your company requires before you ask for her Social Security Number and credit card).

Now, Melissa, the IRS requres that we get your Social Security Number in order to pay you. (Pause. Let her talk. Almost every time I have said it this way, the person immediately gave me their number without comment).

And now I need your credit card information.

If your company requires your new person to sign up themselves online:

Melissa, can you be online right now? Great. Let me give you the site to go to, and I can walk you through the signup process, OK?

Sample Long Form Script

Use this script only if your company or your upline does not have a Recruiting Machine web site to do a power presentation for you. ***This script is incomplete, since you will need to make a presentation yourself. You will need to it script to fit your company***

Hi, Melissa, my name is Bob Sharpe. I'm calling from my home in Duarte, California. You don't know me, but I'm calling because you filled in a form online looking for a way to work from home. My company has a couple openings right now. I'm calling to schedule a short interview with you to see if our company is a good match for you. Is this a good time to talk?

Good. I'd like to start by asking you a few questions to see if we're a good match for you. Then I'll tell you a little about myself and what I do, and you can ask me questions. Is that OK with you?

What's usually better for you, mornings or evenings?

Good. How about if I call you back at 7:00 PM. Would that work for you?

Is this the best number to call?

Great, I'll call back this evening at 7:00 PM.

Be sure to keep your appointment!

- Have you been looking for a home business very long?
- What kind of work do you do now?
- Are you looking for a part-time supplement to your income or a new full-time career?
- If I could show you a business that meets your needs, how soon would you like to get started making money?

Other than the money, what is it that you would like a home business to do for you?

(Let them talk. You want to learn their WHY for having a home business. They are giving you the carrot so you can dangle it in front of them).

1. To be successful, you will need to invest about 7-10 hours a week. Would that work for you?
2. Our business is a people business, and we work with people quite a bit. Do you enjoy working with people?
3. We have found that the people who follow our training very closely are the people who have the best success. Would you consider yourself teachable?
4. Now, Melissa anytime you start up a business, you are going to have startup costs. Our costs are low, and you may qualify to effectively get your startup cost back from the federal government over the first couple of months, .Our normal startup cost is $299. This will cover all (or almost all)[2] the tools you'll be using to make money and the training to use them. If everything else meets your needs, would that fit your budget?
5. What other qualifications do you have that make you believe you could be successful in your own business, working from home?

---

[2] Say what applies to your company's opportunity.

How to Recruit People on the Internet

[Let them talk. If they don't come up with anything, suggest... Are you a hard worker? Easily motivated? Like to help people?]

It sounds like you could be a good fit for our team, and that you are somebody I could get excited about working with.

Let me give you a good overview of our company, how you get paid, and how my team and I will be working with you. If at any time either of us feels this is not a good fit for you, I'll be the first one to say this might not be right for you. Fair enough?

The name of our company is ABC Company. Have you ever heard of us?

Our company markets _____.

By the way, this is not one of those pyramid things where a few people at the top get filthy rich and nobody else makes any money. We have thousands[3] (or hundreds) of people earning $500 to $5,000 per month every month. We also have some who are getting very rich.

We offer simplified step-by-step training and personal mentoring to help you be just as successful as you want to be in the business.

Let me tell you how we get paid.

(Briefly mention your compensation plan here. Don't be too detailed. You just want to give them enough to show them that they can really make money with your company. Experienced network marketers might want more detail. People without experience generally won't understand a lot of compensation plan detail).

Melissa, it starts out small, but it can grow into a huge money machine for you. If you've ever read Rich Dad Poor Dad, this is the type of income he talks about. Would that change your

---

[3] Our hundreds – depends on your company. Give accurate information.

life . . . to have thousands of dollars a month in residual income coming in . . . for the rest of your life?

Skills and Education

Many of the successful people in our business have started fresh – no skills or experience in our business. We give you the education, and we help you develop the skills.

If there's one thing that I really want you to understand, Melissa, it's that being successful in our business is a skill you can learn. If you diligently apply yourself to learning the skill, and if you practice the skill every day, you can learn it too – just as thousands of others have done. Does that make sense to you?

We will teach you...

1. How and where to find people.
2. Exactly what to say to them.
3. How to find people on the Internet.
4. How to use your web site and how to let the tools do much of the work for you.

Many people tell us that they have learned more about earning a big paycheck through our training than they ever learned in their whole lives. And (much of)4 the training – except for the national events – is totally free when you join me in ABC Company

That means this is more than just the best business opportunity. It is a world-class education on financial freedom. How does that sound to you?

Here's the best part...

---

4 Modify for your company. Use "most of" if they have to pay for some of their training.

You can get started for only $299, and you can start making money right away!

Be very confident and do not hesitate when you get to the next part.

Now I need to know . . .

1. How would you like your name printed on your paychecks?
2. And what address would you like your paychecks mailed to?

Finish the questions for the application if your company allows you to take applications over the phone and enter them online. If your company does not allow that, ask them to go to the website so you can walk them through the signup process.

How to ask for their Social Security Number if you are taking their application over the phone:

Now, in order for our company to pay you, the IRS requires that we have your Social Security Number.

(Pause. Wait for them to speak. If you are comfortable, they will usually be comfortable giving it. You'll be amazed at the number of people who will give you their number without making a comment. A few will balk before giving it to you. Very few will refuse. If it is an issue, send them to your web site to sign up online. You can walk them through the process without them giving you their Social Security Number).

If they join... Tell them:

Congratulations, and welcome to our family. Watch your email for a confirmation from the company.

I'll be working with you to help you be successful. (Or, you will be assigned an upline mentor to help you be successful).

What is the dream lifestyle you would like to have when you become very successful in this business?

(Encourage them to talk about their dream. What kind of house they would like to live in, the car they would like, what they would like to do for their children, where they would like to vacation, etc. Help them to realize that today, for the first time in their life, that dream is within reach. They just have to reach out and achieve it in their new business).

How important is that dream to you? If you knew you could have it within a few years, what would you be willing to do to get it?

Network marketing is like life. Sometimes it's easy, sometimes it's hard. The people who are successful got there by sticking to it and doing the things that are important to success every day – even when they didn't feel like it. The people who are making $100,000 a month started the same way you are starting today. If they can do it, don't you think you can do at least 1/10 of that they are doing? If you do, you'll be earning $10,000 a month in residual income. How far would that get you toward your dream?

Other things to tell them

1. Start on their Top 40 List.
2. Show them the back office on the company web site if it is available to them yet.
3. Invite them to the next conference call or webinar from your team or from the company.
4. Schedule a time to meet or call them tomorrow.

If they don't join...

Try to schedule a time to call them again within 24-48 hours.

19 How to Recruit Other Network Marketers

How to Recruit a Person Who is Doing Another Network Marketing Business

First, find out if they are happy in their business. Ask them how long they've been doing it and how well it is working for them. Try to determine if they are really happy in their business and if they are really making money, or if they are faking it.

If they are happy in their business

Realize that you won't recruit them right away, so don't try yet. All you want to do at this point is to subtly get your foot in the door.

Don't get into a debate about which business is better. Befriend them and ask them what they like about their business, and listen. Tell them you're glad they're happy, and that you wish them well.

At that point, they will either try to recruit you, or they will reciprocate and ask you what you like about your business.

If they try to recruit you, tell them that you are focusing on your business and that it really isn't possible to be successful building two network marketing businesses at the same time. Tell them you would like to stay in touch with them, and that from time to time you might want to call them or have coffee with them and share some things you are learning that might be helpful to them in their business. (You are baiting the hook for when they are ready to bite).

If they ask you what you like about your business, pick 2-4 things from this list to share with them (assuming they are true):

1. You are making money.

2. You are getting a lot of personal support from your upline mentor and/or your team leader, and you are learning a lot of good things about being successful in network marketing.

3. You are excited about the system that your company and/or team has put together to help you build your business.

4. Your upline team has helped you with a great source of leads, so you always have people to talk to about your business.

5. You are marketing a Quadrant 1 product that is easy to sell, and that people keep for a long time, giving you an ongoing residual income.

6. You've got a lot of people in your waiting room, and more are coming in all the time.

At this point, don't go into detail unless they start asking a lot of detailed questions.

Most network marketers don't have any of the 6 things listed above and would love to have them. Resist the temptation to do the "my company is better than your company" thing.

Don't be arrogant, but offer to share new things you learn from time to time. Call them in a week and share something you have learned. If nothing else, share something you have learned from this book.

As much as I would love to have you recommend my book to them, you might not want to do it now. That way you have a lot of material to pick from to share with them. You don't have to tell them you got it from me.

If you can impress them with your knowledge and your willingness to help them, they'll call you when they get discouraged with their company or their upline's inability or unwillingness to help. When they do that, they have taken the first step – consciously or unconsciously – toward joining you in your business.

Remember, you can lead a horse to water, but you can't make him drink. Howver, you can make him thirsty. Your job is to make your friend very, very thirsty for the advantages you've got in your company.

Sooner or later, most network marketers get discouraged with their businesses. When that happens to them, you want to be the one they call.

When they're happy with their business, they're not open to yours. When they're unhappy, that's when they'll be open, and you want to be the first person they will call.

If they are not happy in their business

Ask them why they are not happy. Listen to them. This is very important – especially at this point. Show them you care.

If their complaint corresponds to any of the 6 things on the list on the preceding page (it probably does), ask them what their upline's support system is doing to help them. If you uncover a sore spot, you've just moved them one more step toward joining your business.

Offer some encouragement. Then you could say something like this:

I'd really like to help you, and I'll do what I can. I think you understand, however, that there is only so much I can do for you in another business. I'd really like to have you working with me in mine, and I think we would work well together. Would you consider taking a look at what we have to see if it might be a good fit for you?

If they say yes, give them a presentation. Stress the things your company, your upline team and you will do for them that they are not getting in their current company.

Does it work? I know a number of good people who were recruited from other companies with this approach. Some of them became leaders in their new companies.

20 Advertising Your Business

Although advertising can bring you a lot of business, it isn't the magic bullet that conquers all your challenges. A lot of people think they can run an ad and the phone will ring off the hook. It could happen, but all too often people run an ad and the phone doesn't ring at all. That's because they don't know how to advertise effectively, or they place their advertisements in the wrong places.

Like anything else you do in life, advertising is a skill. The people who know how to do it best get the most out of their ads.

Before You Advertise

1. Know how to talk to the people who respond. If you don't know how to give a good presentation yet, don't advertise. You need to know what to say to people when they answer your ad.

2. Know your company's policies and procedures concerning advertising. Some distributors have been kicked out of their businesses for running unapproved ads.
3. Be completely honest in your advertising.
4. Look for free ways to advertise your business
5. Talk to your upline mentor about successful advertising used by people in your company.

Reach Out and Grab Someone

That's what great headlines do. Great headlines evoke curiosity and interest and compel people to begin reading the ad.

The headline of your ad is the most important part. If it doesn't do its job, your ad is worthless. Expensive worthless.

People are preoccupied. Your company, your products and services, are the last things on their minds. They're thinking about themselves, their weekend at the beach and how they're going to pay the bills. You've got to break in with your message, get their attention and then interest them enough to read your ad. That is the job of the headline.

Before you write an ad, grab a newspaper or magazine and read the ad headlines. See how the best headlines try to reach out and grab you.

- **Speak Spanish Like a Diplomat** – *a powerful simile*
- **10 Ways to Beat the High Cost of Living** – *a list of strategies*
- **New Concept in Weight Control** – *something new*
- **The Secret of Making People Like You** – *inside information*

Headline Creator Pro – The Inexpensive Software that writes your headlines before your eyes!

There is an amazing piece of inexpensive software that creates powerful headlines with the click of a mouse. Just enter a few facts about your product or opportunity, click the mouse and voila! You are presented with a big list of powerful headlines you can use for print or online advertising.

You can use it over and over to create powerful headlines any time you want. You can find it in the Resource Section of

www.ITrainMillionaires.com

You-focused, not us-focused

Your ad isn't to tell people about you and your company and how great your company is. They don't care about you and your company. It's about them, their problems and desires, and how your business opportunity can change their lives. It's not about how much money your top earners are making. It's about how ordinary people – like your readers – are changing their lives, and about how they can too. If you don't get that, you'll be lucky if your ad sticks around long enough to line the bottom of the bird cage tomorrow.

Identify a hurt and the solution

People will go to great lengths to get their problems solved. Look at all the money people pay to lose weight. (It's easier to pay a few hundred or a few thousand than it is to change your eating habits, isn't it?). Therapists, psychologists and lawyers can make a bundle by helping people solve their problems.

People are hurting today. They want more and more stuff, and they have less and less money to pay the bills. When they buy some of the stuff they want with credit cards, their financial situations worsen. A lot of people are hurting financially. Most people don't realize this, but if you drive through some of the exclusive neighborhoods in your town, a lot of those people have big financial needs also – on a bigger scale.

Who Are the Most Likely People to Join Your Business? Go There

Address those needs and advertise in the places where your target audience will see your ad.

Most of the people I know who joined a network marketing company and became successful were middle class people – from lower middle to upper middle class. A few lower class people made it, and a few upper class people joined, but the people from both ends of the spectrum were the exceptions. Target the people in the middle. Write your ads for them and place your ads in the places where they will see them.

Where to Advertise

Pay per Click

With this type of advertising, the search engine will display your ad. Every time a person clicks on the ad, they will be taken to your website, and you pay a designated amount. You will pay regardless of whether the person buys or not. It could even be a competitor clicking to see what you're up to. You still pay.

Don't complain about paying for clicks when people don't buy. Only a small percentage of the clicks result in sales. That is normal. At least they looked. If you had your ad in a newspaper, you pay even if they don't look.

Of course you need a number of people to join or buy your product to pay for the advertising and make it profitable. Don't expect the phone to be ringing off the hook. If you place a classified ad in a large newspaper, you might get 3-10 calls, and half of them will be from other people trying to recruit you into their business. It's the law of large numbers. You go through a lot of people to get a few people. In the case of most advertising, which is not personal like personal contacts, you expose your business to a larger number of people to get smaller number of prospects. It's faster and easier to reach masses of people this way, however, so advertising can be an effective way to build your business.

To do this type of advertising you will set up an account with Google or another search engine.

Classified ad publications

Classified ad publications, like the Pennysaver, the Green Sheet and other free classified papers usually are not the best place to advertise your business opportunity, because most of the people that read those types of papers are usually not the best prospects for a network marketing business.

6 Before it Sticks

If you place one ad somewhere, don't expect to get a lot or results from one ad. Most people don't respond until they've had at least 6 exposures to your ad. That's why we say "6 before it sticks."

That's why you see the same TV ads over and over. Watch a 2-hour movie, and you might see the same advertiser's commercials 3 or 4 times or more. Why? Because the advertisers know that you probably won't respond until you have seen their commercial over and over.

If you're thinking of placing an ad, don't do it if you can't afford to run it several times in succession. When I worked in radio, some of the stations sold "saturation packages" of advertising in which they would sell 70 commercials to be run in a 3-day period. Many advertisers found the saturation packages to be very effective because of the power or repetition.

Emotion = Motion

When you advertise, use words that trigger peoples' emotions. All the facts reasons in the world (yawn) won't do much to get most people to take action. Use emotional words and phrases. When you can get the other person to feel something positive about your business, you've got him moving in the right direction,

The Real Reason People Buy

When people respond to an offer, they unconsciously have two reasons for acting. The strongest reason is the emotional reason. They feel it. They want it. Then they really, really, really want it. That's the reason you bought the car you wanted instead of the cheapest car that would get you to work. Didn't it feel good when you bought it?

The Other Reason People Buy

When you went out and bought a new camera, why did you buy it? Really? Is that what you told your spouse? Or did you explain the purchase by saying "we need it so we can get more pictures of the children?"

This is the logical reason. The emotional reason is the real reason people buy. The logical reason is the reason they give to other people to explain why they made the purchase.

That being the case, you want to think of both reasons when you advertise and when you present your business. Hook 'em with emotions, but give 'em a reason to explain it to their spouses.

Advertising Power Words

Now we're ready to look at powerful words you can use in your headlines and your ads. Over the years I have come across 3 lists of power words that make headlines stand out and that make ads effective. There is some overlap in these lists because they came from different sources.

Whenever you write advertising for your business, read through the words on the lists on the following pages. That exercise could get your mind flowing with good advertising ideas.

21 Advertising Power Words

Whenever you write an ad or write copy for a web site or advertising email, you might want to keep these lists in front of you

36 Words that Make People Buy

Free	Sale	How to	Healthy
Love	Now	Discover	Guarantee
Safe	Value	Introduce	Natural
New	Fun	Easy	Fast
Benefits	Save	Your	Precious
Right	Gain	Proven	Secret
You	Money	Penetrate	Solution
Alternative	Happy	Suddenly	Magic
Security	Advice	Proud	Comfortable

108 Power Words That Trigger Results/Action

Abolish	Define	Implement	Refresh
Accelerate	Defuse	Improve	Replace
Achieve	Deliver	Increase	Resist
Act	Deploy	Innovate	Respond
Adopt	Design	Inspire	Retain
Align	Develop	Intensify	Save
Anticipate	Diagnose	Lead	Scan
Apply	Discover	Learn	Segment
Assess	Drive	Leverage	Shatter
Avoid	Eliminate	Manage	Shave-off
Boost	Ensure	Master	Sidestep
Break	Establish	Maximize	Simplify
Bridge	Evaluate	Measure	Solve
Build	Exploit	Mobilize	Stimulate
Burn	Explore	Motivate	Stop
Capture	Filter	Overcome	Stretch
Change	Finalize	Penetrate	Succeed
Choose	Find	Persuade	Supplement
Clarify	Focus	Plan	Take
Comprehend	Foresee	Position	Train
Confront	Gain	Prepare	Transfer
Connect	Gather	Prevent	Transform
Conquer	Generate	Profit	Understand
Convert	Grasp	Raise	Unleash
Create	Identify	Realize	Use
Cross	Ignite	Reconsider	Whittle-down
Decide	Illuminate	Reduce	Win

100 Words that Sell

Absolutely	Fascinating	Miracle	Sensational
Amazing	Fortune	Noted	Simplified
Approved	Full	Odd	Sizable
Attractive	Genuine	Outstanding	Special
Authentic	Gift	Personalized	Startling
Bargain	Gigantic	Popular	Strange
Beautiful	Greatest	Powerful	Strong
Better	Guaranteed	Practical	Sturdy
Big	Helpful	Professional	Successful
Colorful	Highest	Profitable	Superior
Colossal	Huge	Profusely	Surprise
Complete	Immediately	Proven	Terrific
Confidential	Improved	Quality	Tested
Crammed	Informative	Quickly	Tremendous
Delivered	Instructive	Rare	Unconditional
Direct	Interesting	Reduced	Unique
Discount	Largest	Refundable	Unlimited
Easily	Latest	Remarkable	Unparalleled
Endorsed	Lavishly	Reliable	Unsurpassed
Enormous	Liberal	Revealing	Unusual
Excellent	Lifetime	Revolutionary	Useful
Exciting	Limited	Scarce	Valuable
Exclusive	Lowest	Secrets	Wealth
Expert	Magic	Security	Weird
Famous	Mammoth	Selected	Wonderful

22 Business Briefings

Sometimes called *opportunity meetings,* these meetings are usually held in hotels or restaurants. These are meetings where you can take your prospects to hear a presentation on the business opportunity.

Even though a lot of people now prefer using conference calls and webinars, business briefings can be very effective. When your prospect sees a number of people who are earning good incomes in your company, it can make a powerful impression. A good business briefing has a lot of energy that gets prospects emotionally involved in the presentation.

When people face a decision, the way the feel about it is often more powerful than what they know about it. The feeling they get from the energy of the business briefing can go a long way in helping them decide to join your business. If your prospect is sitting on the fence, just the sight of the other people signing up can convince him or here to join too. You cannot duplicate this energy on the Internet or on the phone.

How to Profit the Most from a Business Briefing

When you invite people to a business briefing, don't tell them it is a weekly meeting. If you do, their natural tendency will be to say, "Let me do it another week. I might have something going on this week."

The only meeting you are promoting is this week's meeting. Otherwise many people will put it off until the next week, and the next week, and the next week . . . and keep putting it off week after week, forever.

Invite prospects to come

You have your Top 40 List, right? Call some people on your list and invite them. Business briefings are often more effective when you invite people you have already exposed to the business. If you have already exposed them to your business, you can say...

> Hey, Susie, remember the business I was telling you about? I want to make sure you get enough good information so you can make an intelligent decision. One of my friends, who is doing very well in the business, will be sharing this Thursday evening. I thought this would be perfect for you to see and get your questions answered. Can I stop by and pick you up at 7:00?

If you haven't told them about your business before,

> Hey, Susie, I found something that made me think about you. You know how I've always wanted to make more money? Well, I've found it. I'm working with some successful businesspeople to increase my income. They're

doing a briefing on Thursday evening, and I'd like to introduce you to them to see if it might be something you'd be interested in too. Can I stop by and pick you up at 7:00?

If she asks, "What is it?"

They're helping me start my own business. I plan on being fulltime in a year or so. Rather than trying to explain it myself, I'd like you to meet them and get the whole story. That's why I'd like to pick you up at 7:00. Can you be ready by then?

If she asks, "Is it network marketing?" or MLM, or a pyramid.

Do you mean one of those things where a few people at the top make all the money and all the people at the bottom don't make anything?

It's not like that. It's a different kind of network marketing business. A lot of people are making money soon after they get started, and there are a lot of people making a decent full-time income who haven't made it to the top yet.

Pick them up

When the people you invite to a briefing promise to come, you're lucky if 50% show up. However, in the history of network marketing, 100% of the people picked up for meeting showed up (unless there was an accident on the way).

If you want 100% to show up, pick them up. Your business will grow faster if you do.

Edify the presenter

Be very positive in talking about the presenters and the other leaders who are likely to be at the meeting. Talk about their accomplishments and how joining your company changed their lives. Talk about them as if they walk on water and glow in the dark. Don't say anything negative about the presenter.

5 Minutes before the meeting starts

If your prospect is driving there himself, call him to see how soon he will be there. If he doesn't answer or if he says he will be late, take a seat near the back when the meeting starts and save him a seat.

Sit near the front

Usually the people who are the most interested sit in the 2 front rows of a meeting. Your prospect might be embarrassed to sit in the front row, but row 2 or 3 is a good choice.

In addition, there is more energy in the front of the room, which will add impact to the presentation for your prospect.

And don't forget to turn your cell phone off!

Listen attentively and applaud enthusiastically

You may have heard the presentation 100 times before, but listen attentively as if were you were hearing it for the first time and you were very interested. Pay attention and don't talk. Your body language will send a strong message to your guest about the importance of the presentation.

At the end...
"What did you like best about what you heard?"

Don't ask them what they think about the presentation or the opportunity. Assume that they liked it. Always be very positive. Even if they don't sign up at the briefing, it will be easier to follow up with them if they leave the meeting with positive thoughts in their minds.

What to do if your prospect doesn't show up

Call them, but don't scold them. Let them know they were missed. Your call will give them a little discomfort about not showing up. That's OK. Don't make them feel as if they have to make an excuse for not showing up. MAKE AN EXCUSE FOR THEM! You can say something like this:

Hey Susie, I'm really sorry you weren't able to make it last night. I know something must have come up at the last minute. I understand.

I'd really like to do this another time. Would next Thursday work for you?

Why prospects sometimes don't show up

You place a lot of importance on these meetings. Your prospects won't place nearly as much importance on them. That's natural. It's because they don't know what you know, so they can't be expected to feel what you feel. Don't get discouraged. That's what happens. Just keep moving forward.

People use business briefings because they work. If you use them, they will work for you, too.

Home Meetings

You can also do a business briefing in your home. Invite some people over and do a presentation like the presentations you see in the business briefings.

If you do a home meeting, don't serve a lot of refreshments. Sometimes just a cold drink will do. We suggest clear liquids, like Sprite, 7-Up or lemonade, because if there is a spill it won't make as much of a visible mess to disrupt the meeting. If you feel like you must serve something to eat, make it popcorn or chips without dip or salsa. You should not serve anything that would make a mess and disrupt the meeting if it spills.

23 Natural Laws of Business

1. The Law of Averages

You probably know that most of the people you meet will not want to join your network marketing business. You also know that some people will be interested, and some of them will eventually join. It's usually about 5-10%.

That being the case, you can safely assume that if you give 100 presentations, you will probably have a good chance of having about 10 people interested in your business.

Knowing this, you know that there will always be a percentage of the people you present to who will join.

Keep on finding people to present to. Keep on making presentations. As you do, the Law of Averages says you will get some of them – provided you make a good presentation for a good program.

It's just – the Law of Averages, and over time, it will work in your favor.

2. The Law of Large Numbers

The Law of Large Numbers is somewhat akin to the Law of Averages. It states, "In order to get a small number of people in your downline, you have to make presentations to a large number of people."

Two Types of Expectation

You know going in that some will join and some will not. It's always that way.

1. You have to expect people will join your business when you make a presentation.

When you are giving presentations, proceed as though you expect every person to say yes. After all, who doesn't want to make more money? Who wouldn't want the opportunity to be living the lifestyle of their dreams within a few years? It's logical. It's a no-brainer. You see it. You're on the path to the lifestyle of your dreams, and you'll get there if you keep traveling the path. You expect other people to see it and join you. It's in their best interest.

When you have that kind of expectation, it will affect the words you say and the way you say them. It will give you a contagious positive energy that attracts people to your business and causes them to want to join.

2. You have to expect that most people will not join your business.

This sounds contradictory to the paragraphs above, but it really isn't, because even when you expect your prospects to join, most will do the unthinkable – they won't join. Nobody bats 1000, and you won't either.

So here's how you handle it. Before and during your presentation, you absolutely positively unequivocally expect your prospect to join you in the business, and you give it the best you've got. Your conviction and expectation give power to your presentation. You will recruit more people that way.

If your prospect does the unthinkable and says no, you change your expectation. You change it because of the Law of Large Numbers. You know you have to go through a large number of people in order to get a small number of people into the business.

Knowing the Law of Large Numbers keeps you motivated and on track, because it teaches you that you have go through the many to get the few.

Remember, the more people you present to, the more you will get. The more you present, the better you will get at it, and the more you'll recruit. The tragic thing is that most people quit before they've worked enough in their business to develop their skills.

3. The Law of Failure – When failure isn't failure

"For most people, their fear of failure
outweighs their desire to succeed."
--Les Brown

"It is wise to keep in mind that no success or failure
is necessarily final."
--Anonymous

"Failure is the condiment that gives success its flavor."
--Truman Capote

"Success consists of going from failure to failure
without loss of enthusiasm."
--Winston Churchill

So, how can it be that failure isn't always failure? Isn't that a contradiction? Not at all. There are times when failure becomes a great victory.

When Thomas Edison was in the process of inventing the electric light bulb, he faced constant failure. He tried many different materials as the filament of the bulb. One after another, they didn't work. He kept on working tirelessly.

Someone mentioned that he was failing in his efforts to invent the electric light. He replied, "I have not failed. I've just found 10,000 ways that won't work."

What do you think would have happened had he admitted defeat? He would have stopped working on his project, and somebody else would have become famous for inventing the electric light.

Failure becomes success when you learn the lesson the failure has to teach you, and when your lesson causes you to be successful.

Every time you fail, there is a lesson for you to learn. Learn it and keep on going until you discover the success it is teaching you to find.

"Many of life's failures are people who did not realize how close they were to success when they gave up."
–Thomas Edison

4. The Law of Cause and Effect

"Shallow men believe in luck. Strong men believe in cause and effect."
--Ralph Waldo Emerson

The Law of Cause and Effect states that, in the material world we live in, everything that exists was caused by something or Somebody. The universe exists because it was created. You got a paycheck because you worked for it. You got an A on the exam because you knew the material. Your friend got an F because he didn't study. Every effect has a cause.

In your network marketing business, your success is caused by the things you and your team do. Success doesn't just happen by itself. Nothing just happens by itself.

That being the case, you can cause your own success in your business. More than that, you must cause the success in your network marketing business, or you won't have any. That means you need to learn the simple skills and work hard.

I was visiting with a friend the other day, and he was telling me about an acquaintance. They had been out of touch with for many years, and then reconnected. He was surprised to find that his acquaintance was now earning a multiple 6-figure monthly income in a network marketing business. He now owned a 20,000 square foot house in an exclusive area of Southern California.

When my friend asked how he did it, he replied that he had spent a number of years working 16-hour days to build his network marketing business, and now he was reaping the reward.

Most people who work 16 hour days get overtime. Network marketers get rich.

If you have been working in your network marketing business for some time and you're not making much money, take a look at what you're doing and how you're doing it. That's where you'll find the reason.

If you supply the right cause, you'll get the right effect. It might not happen immediately, but it will happen in time.

If you want massive results, you have to take massive action.

5. The Law of Multiplication

Addition produces small results slowly. Multiplication produces big results fast.

Let's use 5 occurrences of the number 10, as an example.

10   10   10   10   10

Let's take those 5 10's and add them together:

10 + 10 + 10 + 10 + 10 = 50

Now let's take those 5 10's and change their functions:

10 × 10 × 10 × 10 × 10 = 100,000

So, what is the difference between adding the 10's and multiplying them?

It's the difference between 50 and 100,000!

When you add the 10's, you get 50. When you multiply them, you get 100,000. Big difference, isn't it? That's the power of multiplication.

Although wealthy people know ways to multiply their incomes, most people earn their livings with addition. They do things to add to their paycheck, and if they want to make more money, they have to do certain things to add to their income. Learn to earn with multiplication.

How to Be a Network Marketing Millionaire

Making money by addition

- Add more hours to your work schedule
- Add to your paycheck by getting a raise.
- If you're a lawyer, bill more hours
- If you're a salesperson, Sell more stuff
- Or you can add a second job

Addition – that's all that most people know how to do when they want more income.

Making money by multiplication – the secret of the wealthy.

Wealthy people have learned how to increase their income through multiplication.

Look at Henry Ford, for example. How did he get wealthy? It wasn't by building cars. He did not build cars for a living. He built a company that built cars. That's the difference.

If Henry Ford built cars, he could have, perhaps, built 6 or 7 cars a year and made enough to support his family. Instead, he built a company that built millions of cars, making him one of the wealthiest men in the world. **By multiplying his ability to make cars, he multiplied his income thousands of times over.**

You can make a living selling products or services. Millions of people do. You can make infinitely more money by building an organization – a downline – that can sell thousands of times more than you can by yourself. That is the power of multiplication. That is why you can make so much money in network marketing. Very few people embrace it. Those who master it become wealthy.

You had to master certain skills to do your current job. The skills required to harness the power of multiplication in network marketing are probably easier to master than the skills you learned for your current work.

24 How to Help Your New Distributors Get Started

*There is no man living who isn't capable of doing
more than he thinks he can do.*
--Henry Ford

A new distributor is like a baby. They need a lot of care and attention at first. Then, as they mature, they need less care and attention, but they still need a good strong relationship. The real sign of maturity is when they  reproduce and lead their own "offspring" teams.

Your new people need upline help until they are self-sufficient in the basics of the business.

Some of the things you can do:

1. Introduce your new person to your sponsor and your upline mentor. You can do this with a 3-way call.
2. Try to help them get their first paycheck right away.
3. Encourage and help them to qualify for your company's fast start bonus, if your company has one.

If you are new, ask your upline mentor to help your new people or to help you get an upline mentor for them. Otherwise you should be their upline mentor. Your new people need this from their upline mentor:

<u>T</u>raining
<u>E</u>ncouragement
<u>P</u>resentation Help
<u>A</u>ccountability
<u>R</u>ecognition

Just remember the word "TEPAR" to help you remember the 5 areas of support your new team members need in order to be successful in the business.

1. Training

If you are in a good team and a good company, you probably don't have to do much of the training yourself. It is up to you, however to make your new person aware of the training available, to encourage them to take the training and to discuss the training with them.

Be sure to tell them about
1. Your company's training web site
2. Your company's training conference calls and webinars
3. Your company's local training events
4. Your team's training web site
5. Your team's conference calls and webinars
6. Any other training available
7. And of course, buy them a copy of this book!

Stress the importance of the training.

If a surgeon didn't go to medical school, do you think he would be successful? If a person didn't go to law school, do you think she would make a good lawyer? And if you don't go to network marketing "school," do you think you'll make a lot of money in network marketing? Of course not!

The plain truth is that people won't make money in network marketing until they learn how to do it. Duh! The fastest and easiest way to learn is to take the training offered by your team and your company, and then to practice and go to work with it.

Help them learn the presentation and practice with it. Role play with them. Then let them watch and listen as you make presentations with their prospects.

2. Encouragement

"The greatest management principle in the world is
the things that get rewarded and appreciated get done."
-- Michael LeBouef

As human beings, we are all in need of encouragement. Be positive and encouraging whenever you speak with your new business partners. Keep all negative talk and thoughts to yourself.

When they recruit a new person or make a sale, congratulate them – even if you're the one making the presentation with them.

Always make them feel good about their efforts and their successes.

When they are having troubles in the business, encourage them to conquer the difficulties and go forward to the goal of their dream lifestyle. That is what winners do. Expect them to be winners.

3. Presentation Help

When a new person joins, it is important for them to approach the people in their warm market. There is a problem, however. Often, their friends and family won't believe them. "You've gone into business? You don't know anything about that! Why should I believe you?"

Their friends trust them, but they don't believe they know what they are talking about. That's where you come in. You are the expert. Your new distributor partner's friends might not know whether they can trust you or not, but they will have no trouble believing you if their friend tells them you are an expert.

That is how you solve the problem and train your new person at the same time. Your partner introduces you as the expert. You make the presentation and they listen. All the while you are training your new person and you are helping to build their team (and yours).

Let your new person know that you will not always be making their presentations. The purpose of your help is to get them going fast and to train them to do their own. Let them know that they will be learning to do the presentations for their new downline members in the future. That's how a network marketing business grows. You recruit, train and pass along the responsibility.

4. Accountability

Dr. Elmer Towns, of Liberty University, said, "People don't do what you expect; they do what you inspect."

Keep up with the progress your new people are making. Call them to remind them of the conference calls, webinars and meetings. Let them know you are interested in their progress, and that you want to help them achieve their dreams.

You are not their boss. Don't scold them when they miss a conference call. If they grow lax in the business, try to gently nudge them, but don't hound them. Let them know you are interested in them and their future, and that you want them to succeed.

5. Recognition

People thrive on recognition. They love it, and they'll go to great lengths to get it.

If you know your picture is going to be in the paper, how many papers do you buy that day? Everybody loves recognition – even shy people.

When your new person gets their first check, praise them. When they get their first promotion, call them and congratulate them. Ask your upline to call them too. Congratulate them publicly on your conference call or webinar and in your meetings. Then continue to give recognition to your downline business partners each time they make a significant step in their network marketing careers.

25 Problems You Will Face

If everything seems under control,
you're just not going fast enough.
-- Mario Andretti, Race Car Driver

Obstacles are those frightful things you see
when you take your eyes off your goal.
--Henry Ford

Life is a fight for territory.
Once you stop fighting for what you want,
what you don't want will automatically take over.
--Les Brown

Everybody has problems and everybody gets discouraged from time to time. You will too. Here are some of the things you will face. Be prepared. They're coming.

Remember, the people who make it to the top are not the people who don't fall down along the way. They are the people who pick themselves up, learn from the fall and move ahead with a resolve to win. That's the ultimate difference between winners and losers.

The Rule When Dealing With Problems and Discouragements

You must have long-term goals to keep you from being frustrated by short-term failures.
-- Charles C. Noble

I'm never down. I'm either up or I'm getting up.
--Unknown

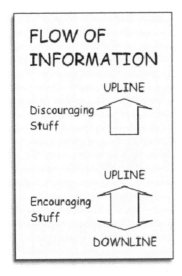

Share your problems and discouragements with your upline to get help. NEVER share them with your downline. You never want to discourage them.

If you get discouraged, or if you hear a bad rumor about your company, if you have a complaint about the company or if you are having a hard time recruiting or selling, tell your upline leader. Never tell your downline.

When you have good news about the company, about the success of a team member, or anything else that is uplifting or encouraging, by all means, share it with your downline. Part of your job is to encourage your team.

When People Say No

*Where would you be today right now
if you let your fears stop you?*
--Maria Holly, speaking to Buddy Holly in the movie,
The Buddy Holly Story

I've Never Had Anyone Say No to Me

I've been successful in network marketing for over 10 years. During that time, I've never had anyone say no to me when I shared my business with them. Not one. It's true. I've never had anyone say no to me.

I've had many people say no to themselves, no to their futures, no to their incomes, no to their families and no to their dreams. They have said no to themselves, not to me. I don't have to live with their unfortunate decisions. They do. I can move on.

When you have something valuable to offer, nobody ever says no to you. They are not rejecting you. They are rejecting their opportunity to have something better in life. You can move on to find the right people for your business. The people who say no will remain stagnant for the rest of their lives.

Most people will never see it. Most people will never join your business. It's a given. On the other hand, some will. You have to go through the no's to find the yeses.

A number of years ago, an insurance company came up with a way to train its new agents. Many agents had quit before they earned any money because they got discouraged from all the people they talked to who weren't interested.

The company management announced that they were going to offer a $1,000 bonus to all new agents who qualify.

They then handed them a sheet of paper that was divided up into 1,000 boxes.

"Every time you try to set an appointment or make a presentation and the prospect says no," the manager explained, "mark an 'X' in one of the boxes. When you get 1,000 no's, you will have all 1,000 boxes filled. Turn in the paper, and we'll give you a $1,000 bonus."

Suddenly the new agents didn't dread the no's any more. Each time they got a no, they smiled, marked the box and went on to find another prospective client.

What do you think happened when they talked to that many people? They sold insurance. Lots of insurance. It got them to see that selling is not convincing people to buy what they don't want. It's finding the right people and helping them to get what they DO want.

Now probably nobody is going to offer you $1,000 to collect 1,000 no's. Go get them anyway, because in the process you'll recruit new people and make money. The experience you get and the progress you make will get you well on your way to a lifetime of success in your business.

Getting 1,000 no's can change your life forever!

How to Handle Objections

*"Too bad all the people who know how to run the country
are busy driving taxicabs and cutting hair."*
--George Burns

Don't be afraid of objections. Often they are the prospect's way of saying, "I'm not convinced yet. This is what you need to show me so I can be convinced."

Many times people don't tell you the real reason they are hesitating. It's easier to throw up an objection.

Whenever you encounter an objection, it is probably for one of these reasons:

1. They are interested, but they are not convinced yet.
2. They don't have the money to join, but they don't want to tell you.
3. They are unsure of the potential of the business.
4. They are unsure of themselves and their ability to be successful in the business.
5. They are being influenced by wrong or incomplete information they believed before talking to you.
6. They are negative about everything.
7. They are just not interested. (Don't assume that too early, or you could lose a good person).

I don't have the time

What if you could get other people to do most of the work of building your business?

This is the perfect opportunity for you then. Our business is specifically designed for people who don't have the time.

You can be successful by working just a few hours a week and build it, because as you grow, other people will be doing most of the work to build your business. You won't have to pay them. It's just the way this business works. You will be getting paid for the work they are doing, as well as for the work you are doing.

It's like saving for retirement. You put some money away, even though it seems as if you can't afford it. Why do you do that? So that someday, when you are old, you'll have money to live on.

With this you take a little time, even though it seems like you can't spare it. You do it so in a few years – before you are old – you can have all the time and the money you want. If you could have that in a few years, would it be worth turning the TV off and budgeting your time a little bit for a few years?

I'm not interested

You can ask, "Really? Could you please tell me… is it the money to get started? Or is it that you're just not interested in residual income?"

Let them talk. Then bring them back to the residual income.

A lot of times when people say this, it's just a smoke screen to throw you off. Don't take it at face value at first until you probe a bit.

I want to think about it

When people tell you this, they are not telling you they are going to go home and think about it. They are going home to forget about it.

Don't take this excuse at face value. Start asking questions. You can say something like this:

"Really? There's really not that much to think about. I know the residual income you can get will change your life, and think we both know you would like that. I must have not explained something clearly. Exactly what is it you would like to think about before you get started?"

Keep answering their questions or objections until they don't have any left. Then you can ask them, "Is there any reason you would not want to have a large residual income from your own home business?

Hand them an application and say, "Let's get the paperwork out of the way so we can start your training and earning right away."

I don't see myself doing this business

"Really? Why not? Is the residual income potential too low?"

They may tell you they don't see themselves selling your products, or they don't see themselves as salespeople.

"You know, most of us were just like you. We didn't see ourselves doing this business either. When we saw the lifestyle we can have after a few years, we jumped on board. Don't you agree that life is too short and too important to not have what you could have? Look, I'm going to help you get it going, so we'll be doing it together."

Hand them an application. "Let's get your training started so we can help you get your income going.".

I'm not a salesperson

"Perfect. Our business is actually designed for the non-salesperson. That's why so many non-salespeople are making money with us. I'm really glad you brought that up. I'd sure hate to see you miss out on this opportunity because you thought you had to be a salesperson."

Hand them an application. "Let's get you started then. I'll be working with you to help you get your business off the ground."

How much money are you making in the business?

Those of us who have enjoyed an above average network marketing income love answering that question. We love to tell how it changed our lives.

If you're not making money yet, don't be evasive. Answer the question head on with confidence. Don't make excuses.

What to say if you're not making any money

I'm still in training, and I'm not making much yet. My mentor, however, is making a lot of money, and she is training me to make as much as she is and more. Would you be interested in generating a large stream of residual income too?

If you are making a small part-time check:

I'm working 6 hours a week, and I'm making enough for a car payment (or house payment, etc.)." I know I'm not getting rich yet, but it's residual income, so if I take a vacation for 2 months, I still get it. Every month I add a little to my check. All I have to do is continue what I'm doing, and I'll be over $10,000 a month in a few years. Would you be interested in having something like that?

If they say no when you ask them about residual income:

What are YOU doing for residual income?

If they say they are not doing anything for it… Ask WHY NOT?

Why do I have to pay to go to work?

"This is your own business, and not just a job. Any time you start a business, you have to invest something to get it going. It's an investment in your future. The company is using your money to give you (list the things they will get when they start in your company). It's easy to make that money back quickly, and you'll be in profit. Not only that, you may qualify to get your money effectively reimbursed by the government when you start. Does that make sense to you?"

If they continue, you can follow up with, "You know, when you have a job, it's usually free to start, unless you have to buy special tools or clothes, but all you get is a chance to work for the rest of your life, hopefully. When you start your own business, you have a far greater earning potential. Is it worth it to spend a little startup cost to have that?"

If they continue, you can say, "Have you ever considered what it costs to start a business? Most busienesses cost anywhere from $20,000 to over a million dollars to start. Here you can start for only $____, and your earning potential is the same or greater. Don't you agree this is a lot better than 20 Grand or more?"

Finish by saying, "Let's get you started quickly so you can get your investment back fast."

I don't have the money

You can say, "Please tell me. Is it really because you don't have any money, or is it because you're skeptical?" (Most of the time they will tell you it's because they're skeptical).

What is it you're skeptical about? The making money part, or the products?

Many times you can help them through their skepticism once you bring it out into the open. When you discover what they are really skeptical about, you can use the "Feel, Felt, Found" formula:

You can say, "I understand how you feel. I felt that way to, but I found that ..." (fill in the blank with an answer that is applicable to you and/or your company).

I'm not interested in the products

Note: If you are selling a Quadrant 1 product, you probably won't hear this objection very often.

You can ask, "What is it you're not interested in – using them or selling them?"

Once they answer, you can ask:. "Would you be interested in having a home business that would generate enough residual income to change your life?"

If they say yes, say, "The products are just a vehicle to help us get what we really want – the residual income to change our lives. We spend a few hours a week talking about the business and the products, and we spend years enjoying the time and money freedum the residual income brings. Could you be interested in that?

If your business deals with Quadrant 1 products, explain that you've carefully chosen the easiest type of products to build a large residual income. They might not be the sexiest, but they're the easiest. Then you can tell them the reasons:

1. You don't have to convince people they need them.
2. Almost everybody is going to buy them, either from you or someone else.
3. They are consumable, so repeat business is automatic.
4. That makes it easier to do than most businesses.

I don't need the products

If your products are Quadrant 1 products, you can assure your prospect that most people need and use the products. Even if they don't have a need for your Quadrant 1 products (which is highly unlikely), you can assure them that most people do need your products. They probably know that already.

If you are marketing a Quadrant 2 product, explain that there is a some people considers the products to be essential and that you can find them and market the products to them.

That's another reason I love working in Quadrant 1. Not only is it easier to sell the products, it is easier to recruit.

The products are too expensive

Most of the products I have seen that are marketed by network marketing companies are very good quality, and quality usually costs more.

Sell value. Some people will buy value over price – especially when they personally are not affected by the bad economy.

Learn the benefits of paying the premium price for your products and services and learn how explain them convincingly without being too detailed and without hype.

Even if your prospects are convinced yours are better, you may find they are content with the lesser-priced products. Cadillacs are better than Fords and Chevrolets, but Fords and Chevrolets outsell Cadillacs 50 to 1. Why? Because Fords and Chevrolets don't cost as much.

It costs too much to join your business

What if I could show you how can get your money back and get into profit quickly? In addition to that, what if I could show you how you probably qualify for the Government to effectively reimburse you for the cost of starting and building your business monthly or quarterly?

If your company has a way to do this, you could also add

Some people put the start up cost on a credit card, work fast and make enough money to pay the credit card bill before the bill comes in the mail. Would you like to see how we can make that happen for you?

(If you use this approach, you need to know exactly what a new person must do in the first month to make it happen. It would also help if you can tell your prospect that you did it yourself, or about people you know who did it).

If they still object ...

The typical business owner spends $10,000 to $100,000 or more to start a new business, and they never have a chance to earn residual income. It is very rare that anyone is ever able to start their own business without investing something, and the investment with us is about as low as it can get. Does that make sense to you?

I tried network marketing and failed

Failure is simply the opportunity to begin again,
this time more intelligently.
--Henry Ford

Would you like to know the reasons most people fail, why some people succeed, and why you can build your own success?

1. They don't get trained, so they don't even know how to do the things that bring network marketing success.
2. They don't have a good upline mentor to help them through the tough spots so they can start making money.
3. They don't commit themselves to work 5-10 hours a week so they can achieve the lifestyle they want.
4. They never learned how to find interested prospects and how to interest them in the business.
5. They were not in a Quadrant 1 company.

I tried your company and failed

Unless you're willing to have a go, fail miserably,
and have another go, success won't happen.
--Phillip Adams

Really? I'd like to know about your experience.
1. How much of the training did you complete?
2. Did you have an upline mentor to help you get started?
3. How many presentations were you making every week?
4. How long did you continue making presentations every week before you quit?

5. How many people did you bring to the meetings or conference calls?
6. If I can provide an upline mentor to work with you and help you get going in the business to help you make money, is there any reason you wouldn't you be interested?

If they answered no to any of the questions, you can say,

That's the reason so many network marketers fail. We are very committed to helping our team members succeed in the business. You would like to succeed this time, wouldn't you?

(Note: in this conversation you are telling them you are assuming they want to join and succeed. That's the message you want to get across).

I know someone in your company, and if I join, I'll join under them.

You could say, "That's a great idea – if they're successful in the business, and if they and their team is a committed to your success as we are, take a look at them. If they're not, I'd think twice about joining them – even if they're a good friend.

"Very few people make it in the business without a good upline mentor, so make sure you are not jeopardizing your future by choosing someone who can't help you succeed."

You might want to give or lend your prospect a copy of this book so they can learn the importance of being on a team that can help them to success.

I have to talk to my spouse.

You could say, "That's a great idea! A lot of couples work together in the business. And, in a lot of homes, just one partner works in the business with a supportive spouse.

"It would be unfair of me to expect you to remember all the important details to tell him (her) and to be able to answer all the important questions he (she) might have.

Is he (she) there now so we can talk?"

If the spouse is not home...

"When will he (she) get home today so we can get him (her) on the phone?"

Is this one of those pyramid businesses?

By pyramid, do you mean the type of operation where everybody tries to recruit all the people they can so the people at the top can get rich, and where all the people at the bottom don't make any money?

Actually, very business in the world looks like a pyramid. The people at the top make more money than the people at the bottom. And there are a whole lot more people at the bottom than there are at the top. Is it like that at the company where you work?

The people at the top of any business make most of the money. In our business, you have a great opportunity to get to the top. In fact, we're not a pyramid, because we have a lot of people at the top making a lot of money, and we have a lot more people moving there all the time.

1. You, too can make it to the top in a few years
2. When you get part way to the top you can still make a lot of money, even if you never get to the top.
3. You can get residual income
4. You can do it part time while you keep your regular job
5. Many people in this business still work part time hours even when they quit their jobs and go 'full time.'
6. Does that appeal to you?

Hitting the Wall

When I thought I couldn't go on, I forced myself to keep going. My success is based on persistence, not luck.
--Estee Lauder

The pro is the person who has all the hassles, obstacles, and disappointing frustrations that everyone else has, yet continues to persist, does the job, and makes it look easy.
-- David Cooper, Sales Trainer

A champion is one who gets up even when he can't.
-- Jack Dempsey,
Heavyweight Boxing Champion

Some time after you get started in the business, you will get to a point where you feel you can't go on. People aren't listening to you. They're not joining. They're not buying your product or service. It just isn't happening for you. It's just too difficult for you to go on.

The term hitting the wall comes from marathon runners who often experience a time in their race where they feel like they just can't go any further, and they feel the overwhelming urge to quit the race.

One marathon runner described it this way:

"It felt like an elephant had jumped out of a tree onto my shoulders and was making me carry it the rest of the way in.[1] "

Some runners say they can't feel their feet at all. Thought processes get fuzzy. Muscle coordination diminishes, and self-doubt makes the entire race seem futile.

You will hit the wall

In network marketing, when you hit the wall, you'll feel like you're at a dead end. There is nothing you can do to succeed in the business. You're ready to throw in the towel and walk away from your financial investment and the time you put into training and working the business. It gets so bad you'll feel your only option is to quit.

Know what to do when you hit the wall

Hold on! Not so fast! Almost every successful network marketer has hit the wall at least once in his or her network marketing career. The successful people learned what to do when they hit the wall. Those who didn't, well, they are the people who failed.

---

[1] Dick Beardsley, speaking of hitting "The Wall" at the second marathon of his career, the 1977 City of Lakes Marathon.

Make the right decision when you hit the wall

The web site, www.marathonandbeyond.com, gives the best strategy for marathon runners about handling the wall when they hit it. The same holds true for network marketers.

> Athletes who achieve their peak performance usually experience something that has come to be known as "flow," . . . Flow is "a state of consciousness where one becomes totally absorbed in what one is doing, to the exclusion of all other thoughts and emotions," . . . "So flow is about focus."[1]

What happens when you hit the wall

Your focus shifts. When you started, you were focusing on the lifestyle you wanted to achieve – the residual income, the time freedom, your dream life. You were working toward it. It was worth the sacrifice you were making. You knew you were going to accomplish it in time, and it was so valuable to you that you would do anything and everything you could possibly do to achieve it.

You were looking beyond the difficulties and sacrifices necessary because your dream lifestyle was that important.

After a few bumps and turns in the road, however, your focus changed. You became so focused on the aches and pains of building your business in the early stages that you lost sight of your dream.

---

[1] www.marathonandbeyond.com/choices/latta.htm

The athletes who achieved peak performance were in a state of flow, "the state of consciousness where one becomes totally absorbed in what one is doing, to the exclusion of all other thoughts and emotions."

What to do when you hit the wall

1. Call your upline mentor fast. Share your feelings and ask for help and encouragement.
2. Realize that this is a common occurrence, and that successful network marketers are the ones who learned to conquer it.
3. Realize that if others can do it, you can too. You're no different. Some others probably had it worse than you, and they conquered.
4. Know that the wall is a temporary challenge, and that it gets easier on the other side.
5. Remind yourself of your dream, and focus on it in your mind and in your conversation.
6. Do not tell your downline. You don't want them discouraged. If they sense something is wrong, just tell them you're not feeling too well, and you'll be feeling better soon. Otherwise don't say anything.
7. Read a good encouraging book or listen to a great motivational speaker. You can get more information about his material and other great resources at www.ITrainMillionaires.com.

Someone once said, "Tough times never last, but tough people do." Get tough. Face the challenge. Get help from your upline and from good authors and speakers. Focus on what you want in life and not on how you feel right now. You can do it! Do it! You'll thank yourself for the rest of your life.

If you aren't making money in your business

Ask yourself these questions:

1. How many hours a week am I spending on my business?
2. How many of those hours are spent finding people to talk to and making presentations?
3. Am I able to give a logical and convincing presentation?
4. How many presentations am I making every week?
5. How many business briefings did I go to in the past month? How many people did I invite? How many did I bring?
6. How much of the training have I completed?
7. Am I working with your upline mentor?
8. Can I give a simplified explanation of my company's compensation plan to my prospects?
9. How many people are on my Top 40 List?
10. How many of those people have I contacted?
11. Have I called my upline mentor for help?

26 Feeding Your Mind

You become what you think about all the time
-- Earl Nightingale

Your mind is an amazing thing. It is the command center of your life. The ideas you put into it, and the thoughts it generates control your actions and feelings. You can feed it anything you want. You can't, however, feed it trash and expect it to produce lofty thoughts and direct your life in pure and productive actions.

In the early days of personal computers, we used to hear the term GIGO. It stood for Garbage In Garbage Out. You can't put bad stuff in and expect to get good stuff out. Your mind works the same way.

Successful People Feed their Minds on Mind Food

You become what you think about all the time. You think about the things you put into your mind. Some people spend a lot of time learning about movie stars and sports teams. There's nothing wrong with that, but how will it help you change your life and achieve the lifestyle of your dreams?

How to Be a Network Marketing Millionaire

When you feed your mind with the motivational and instructional materials that help you expand your ability to grow and earn, you change your life forever.

A number of years ago I was at the convention of a large network marketing company. As the keynote speaker spoke, he mentioned the C.E.O. of the company.

"I know why your C.E.O. is so successful," he said. "When he picked me up at the airport, I looked in the back seat of his car. It was covered with motivational tapes and tapes of sales and business training. He told me he always listens to them when he's in his car."

Feed your mind on success. As you grow personally, you expand your ability to build your business. You will learn how to make more money in less time. You will learn how to retire earlier with more income.

Brian Tracy said that the average person can get the equivalent of a 4-year college education in 2.6 years by listening to the right stuff on his or her commute to and from work.

Readers are leaders! How much do you read? If you've gotten this far in this book, congratulations! You've already demonstrated that you are interested in going further in life than most people. But don't stop here.

Personally, I listen to more books than I read. I fill my iPod with books and motivational speakers and listen to them whenever I can. I have a small battery-operated speaker I connect to my iPod and I carry it around the house with me when I'm not doing something else that I have to engage my mind in. I listen in the shower. I listen when I'm getting dressed. I listen when I'm washing the dishes (Yup, I do that in our house). I listen when I'm driving. By listening while I'm doing other things, I find I can listen 1-2 hours a day without taking any time out of my schedule. I even learned to speak some basic Chinese this way. Really. 真的

When I was growing up in Michigan, the Michigan Milk Producers Association ran ads with the headline, *"You Never Outgrow Your Need for Milk."* I'd like to rephrase it.

You Never Outgrow Your Need for Growth.

I usually listen to several books per month. I listen to books on personal development, success, marketing, motivation, sales, leadership, internet business, history and biography. I also listen to a lot of Christian books and the Bible, which I recommend highly.

Find a list of my recommended books and other audio trainings in the Resource section of

www.ITrainMillionaires.com

27 How Many Network Marketing Businesses Can You Do at a Time?

Sometimes unsuccessful network marketers feel they can build two or three network marketing businesses at the same time. It's a big mistake.

You can't build 2 network marketing companies at the same time

There is more money to be made by moving toward the top in one network marketing company than by getting half way there in two companies.

You can only focus on one network marketing company at a time.

If you are trying to build two businesses, you will always have a dilemma when you have a prospect to recruit. Which company will you present? If you try to present both companies to a prospect, you lose credibility.

You can do two network marketing companies at the same time, but don't try to build both

If you really love the products of a non-Quadrant 1 network marketing company, go ahead and sign up to be a distributor. You'll save money on the products. If you know people who would be interested in the products too, share them. Other than that, don't tell anyone you are in that company. Over a period of time you might get a few people whose business will pay for your products. If you don't, that's OK, because you are building a fortune with your Quadrant 1 company.

28 Should I Lead With the Opportunity or Product?

You know by now where the money is in network marketing. It's not in sales. It's not in recruiting. It's in building a team of people that make a large number of sales collectively. In that sense you'll make a lot more by recruiting than by selling. However, you can recruit a million people and never make money until they either sell products or buy them.

In order to make money, then, you must do both. When you meet a new prospect, you want to do business with them, one way or the other. I have had many customers who have no interest in network marketing at all, but they bought from me. Eventually, some of them join to do the business. If they don't, that's OK, because they're still customers.

Some people are entrepreneurial. They are a lot more interested in doing a good business and making money than they are in the products. The products are only a vehicle to get them the residual income they want. That's OK too.

The rule of thumb, then, is to approach the person with whatever you think they will be most interested in. You just want to get them in one way or the other.

If they become customers and like the product or service, ask for referrals. If they give you some referrals, you can ask them, "Would you rather have me get the commission for them, or would you rather take the commission yourself?'

If you're talking to a businessperson you just met at a chamber of commerce mixer or breakfast meeting, you probably want to lead with the product. Businesspeople and salespeople who attend are there to find customers for their products and services, and they are open to learning about the products and services you have to offer. They are not there to learn about business opportunities.

While you are getting to know the people at the chamber event, you will meet some people who could be open to your business opportunity. These people fall into two categories:

1. Sales representatives
2. Businesspeople whose product or service is related to yours. For example, if you are selling nutritional products, a chiropractor could be interested in becoming a distributor.

For those people, you could introduce the product and then mention you are looking for representatives.

To be successful in your business, learn to approach people and present both ways.

29 Guaranteed Income

There is no reason you can't be the next network marketing superstar! It's just a matter of learning the skills, going to work and giving your business time to grow.

Of course network marketing companies cannot guarantee you will make any money, but you can.

In the end, you are the guarantee of your own success. You must take responsibility for where you will go in life. God gave you the raw material. You will become what you make of it.

Are you proactively working on building the lifestyle you've always dreamed about? Network marketing is the very best way most people can have it.

Just learn the skills. Go to work. Don't quit. Keep doing it until you have the lifestyle of your dreams.

Who knows? Maybe we'll meet in some exotic part of the world someday. When we do, I'd love to hear your story.

So go ahead. Guarantee your own success. Start now and go get it!

30 Tentmaking

This chapter is especially for people involved in Christian ministry, and are looking for a way to support themselves in their work for God. I am an ordained minister. As much as I love network marketing and what it can do for people, my main passion is serving God and helping people know Him. If you are not involved in ministry, you probably won't need the material in this chapter.

Many years ago I conducted a week of meetings in a large church in Indiana. The associate pastor gave us a gallon bottle of aloe vera juice, which is good for the digestive system. He told me that he was working for the Lord in the church full time without pay, because he was living on residual income from his network marketing business

He was very low-key in his approach. He said he would be happy to show me the business if I was interested and God was leading us in that direction. He made it clear that the bottle of juice was his gift to us whether or not we were interested.

It is a well-known fact among Christians that the Apostle Paul sometimes worked a secular job to support himself during his missionary travels. Although he was highly educated, he worked as a maker of tents. That's why we use the word *tentmaking* to describe the secular work of a bivocational minister or missionary.

I spent much of my adult life as an evangelist, a pastor, and a church planter in the US and Canada. I never got paid much in the ministry, and much of the time I had to do secular work to support my family and ministry. I have done such things as working as a DJ at a local radio station, post card photographer and running a one-man advertising business while I was in ministry positions.

I always liked the idea of running my own home-based business, because my time was flexible for the ministry.

I was always afraid of doing network marketing as a pastor, however, because I didn't want the people in my church and community to think I was looking to recruit them. I wanted to be known as one thing to my congregation and community – a man of God. I also didn't want network marketing going on in the church. I have a firm cmmitment that the church is the place for equipping God's people to serve Him – not to build a network marketing business.

During most of the time I was a bivocational pastor, I ran an advertising business from my home. I made a few things clear to my congregation about my business, then I stopped talking about my business almost completely.

1. I let them know what my business was, and what I did for other businesses.
2. I told them I would never solicit their business. I was their pastor, and I did not expect them to become my customer unless they really wanted to.
3. I told them I would appreciate their business and referrals if they wanted to.
4. I told them that, if they went to my competitor and not to me, I would not have hurt feelings, I would not expect them to give me a reason, and my relationship to them as their pastor would not change.

There was only one time I didn't follow one of those principles. I had a member who owned a business that was having problems. He really needed help, and he was not getting it. I knew I could help him. One day I stopped by his store and said, "Frank, I feel weird doing this, because I had promised you and the other members that I wouldn't solicit your business. However, I think I've got some ideas that you need that could help your business."

"I really need help," he said, emphatically.

"That's why I came by," I answered.

In short, he became my customer, and my advertising stuff really worked for him. I made a little money. He made a lot more money than I did. That's the way I wanted it.

Frank (not his real name) was very happy that I went beyond my business principle. He knew I did it for him, and not for my profit. His business, which was losing money, became profitable.

I'm glad I did it. He's really glad I did it, and nobody in the church faulted me for helping him.

The Internet Changed Everything

In the early 2000's, two of my colleagues and I developed an automated online system for acquiring and processing Internet leads. We bought inexpensive leads from reputable leads dealers. Soon we had thousands of people standing in line to hear about our business. Most of the people were not good prospects, but there were enough good ones to make it very profitable. We spent a few evenings and Saturday mornings calling the leads and helping them get started in the business.

Most of the leads were from other States. That was fine, because we were learning how to use the Internet and cheap long distance calls for recruiting and training. Unlimited long distance was not available then, as it is now.

Using the Internet, you can build a thriving network marketing business and most of the people in your community will never know you are doing it. If they do, it won't affect your potential local ministry, because you are not going around recruiting local people into your business.

If I Were a Bivocational Pastor Today

I would definitely build a network marketing business using the Internet. It wouldn't be immediate income, so I would have to have some other income while building it.

Once you get the residuals rolling in, you can maintain a good full-time income for just a few hours of secular work per month, and you could do it from anywhere – even China!

If you know other bivocational ministers, they might be good prospects for you to share the business with, just as the minister in Indiana shared his with me.

Appendix

Favorite Success Quotes

LESSONS ON LIFE
by Jim Rohn

There are half a dozen things that make 80% of the difference.

The difference between triumphant success or bitter failure lies in the degree of our commitment to seek out, study and apply those half-dozen things

1. LEARN TO BE HAPPY

- Happiness is activity with purpose.
- It's love in practice.
- It's both a grasp of the obvious and the mysterious.

2. DISCIPLINE YOURSELF

- Discipline is the most critical ingredient for success.
- It's the master key that unlocks the door to wealth and happiness
- the glue that binds inspiration to achievement
- the bridge between thought and accomplishment.
- We must all suffer from one of two pains:
- The pain of discipline or the pain of regret.
- The difference is discipline weighs ounces while regret weighs tons.

3. EMBRACE CHANGE

- Unless you change how you are, you'll always have what you've got.

- You can change all things for the better when you change yourself for the better.
- You cannot change your destination overnight, but you can change your direction.

4. LIVE WELL.

- Don't just learn how to earn; learn how to live.
- The good life is not an amount; it is an attitude, an act, an idea, a discovery.

5. REMEMBER ALWAYS...

- Life is worthwhile if you TRY.
- Try to make progress.
- Try your best.
- Life is worthwhile if you GIVE.
- Giving starts the receiving process.
- Life is worthwhile if you PLAN.
- Design your own life or someone else will.
- Let others lead small lives, but not YOU.
- Let others argue over small things, but not YOU.
- Let others cry over small hurts, but not YOU.
- Let others leave their futures in other peoples' hands, but not YOU.

"If you don't design your own life plan, chances are you'll fall into someone else's plan. And guess what they have planned for you? Not much."

—Jim Rohn: Author and motivational speaker

"The road to success is paved with the bricks of failure."
--Bob Sharpe

"Most people wait for things to happen. Winners make things happen."
--Bob Sharpe

"Fortune favors the bold."
--Unknown

"People with goals succeed because they know where they're going"
-- Earl Nightingale, Motivational Speaker

"Of course the rich get richer. They know how to do it, and they act on that knowledge."
--Bob Sharpe

"When times are good, be happy; but when times are bad, consider: God has made the one as well as the other."
—Ecclesiastes 7:14

"The world hates change, yet it is the only thing that has brought progress."
—Charles Kettering

"I will prepare, and someday my chance will come."
-- Abraham Lincoln, 16th President of the United States

"Life brings you opportunities and we do our best to avoid them! Go with life instead."
—Paul Lowe

"Professional sales is not something you do TO people; it's what you do FOR people."
--Bob Sharpe

"If you can dream it, you can do it. Always remember this whole thing was started by a mouse."
-- Walt Disney, Animator, Film Producer

"Success is a choice. It's always your choice."

"A woodpecker can peck 20 times on 1,000 trees and get nothing, but stay very busy. Or he can peck 20,000 times on one tree and get dinner."
--Seth Godin, The Dip

Is what I'm doing worth trading my life for?

"The only way to improve your quality of life is to improve yourself."
-Dr. John Maxwell

"If a person will spend one hour a day on a topic, for five years, he will become an expert."
--Earl Nightingale

"Failure can either make you better or bitter. The choice is yours.
--Dr. John Maxwell

"Do you want success? Choose personal goals over immediate pleasure."
--Dr. John Maxwell

"I never tried quitting, and I never quit trying."
-- Dolly Parton, Entertainer

"Wisdom is a fountain of life to him who has it."
--Proverbs 16:22

"Heroism consists of hanging on one minute longer."
-- Norwegian Proverb

"The most common commodity in this country is unrealized potential."
- Calvin Coolidge

"Successful people do what unsuccessful people are unwilling to do."
--Unknown

"Nothing is more expensive than a missed opportunity."
-- H. Jackson Brown, Author

"Go out on a limb - that's where the fruit is"
-- Will Rogers, Humorist

"Even if you're on the right road, you'll get run over if you just sit there."
--Will Rogers

"You can't build a reputation on what you're going to do."
--Henry Ford

"You miss 100% of the shots you never take."
--Wayne Gretzky

"You will be more disappointed by the things you didn't do than by the ones you did. Explore. Dream. Discover."
--Mark Twain

"Invest in yourself. It is the best investment you will ever make."

"If you're not getting better, you're getting worse."
- Pat Riley, basketball coach

"Success is to be measured not so much by the position that one has reached in life as by the obstacles which he has overcome."
-- Booker T. Washington, Educator

"He who is not courageous enough to take risks will accomplish nothing in life."
-- Muhammad Ali, World Heavyweight Boxing Champion

"Sales is not convincing people to buy what they don't want. It's helping people get what they DO want."
--Bob Sharpe

"The reason most people don't succeed in life is not because they aim too high and miss, but because they aim too low and hit it, or they don't aim at all."
--Les Brown

"You don't get in life what you want. You get in life what you are."
--Les Brown

"You become what you think about all the time."
--Earl Nightingale

"All of us are self-made, but only the successful will admit it."
--Earl Nightingale

"Your mind is a machine. You must program it for success."
--Earl Nightingale

"Most people fail because they don't know that they don't know when they think they know."
--Les Brown

"You are willing to leave your comfort zone when the alarm rings on Monday morning, and when you have to complete an unpleasant task at work. Why then, aren't you willing to leave your comfort zone to learn and do the things that will change your life forever?"
--Bob Sharpe

How to Be a Network Marketing Millionaire

"Life is more than working a job where they pay you just enough to keep you from quitting, and you work just hard enough to keep from getting fired."
--Les Brown

"You fail your way to success."
--Les Brown

"For most people, their fear of failure outweighs their desire to succeed."
--Les Brown

"Act as though it is impossible to fail."
--Anonymous

"Choice, not circumstances, determines your success."
--Anonymous

"In order to succeed, you must first be willing to fail."
--Anonymous

"It is wise to keep in mind that no success or failure is necessarily final."
--Anonymous

"Life's real failure is when you do not realize how close you were to success when you gave up."
--Anonymous

"Success: willing to do what the average person is not willing to do."
--Anonymous

"Success is a state of mind. If you want success, start thinking of yourself as a success."
--Dr. Joyce Brothers

To respond is positive, to react is negative.
--Zig Ziglar

"It's not what you know. It isn't even who you know. It's who knows you that makes the difference."
--Bob Sharpe

"Finally, brethren, whatever things are true, whatever things are noble, whatever things are just, whatever things are pure, whatever things are lovely, whatever things are of good report, if there is any virtue and if there is anything praiseworthy— meditate on these things."
--Philippians 4:8

"It takes 20 years to make an overnight success."
--Eddie Cantor

"Failure is the condiment that gives success its flavor."
--Truman Capote

How to Be a Network Marketing Millionaire

"Destiny is not a matter of chance, it is a matter of choice; it is not a thing to be waited for, it is a thing to be achieved."
--Winston Churchill

"In order to succeed you must fail, so that you know what not to do the next time."
--Anthony D'Angelo

"Many of life's failures are people who did not realize how close they were to success when they gave up."
--Thomas Edison

"The great dividing line between success and failure can be expressed in five words: "I did not have time."
--Franklin Field

"Twelve Priceless Qualities of Success:
1. The value of time.
2. The success of perseverance.
3. The pleasure of working.
4. The dignity of simplicity.
5. The worth of character.
6. The power of kindness.
7. The influence of example.
8. The obligation of duty.
9. The wisdom of economy.
10. The virtue of patience.
11. The improvement of talent.
12. 12. The joy of originating."
--Marshall Field

"Failure is success if we learn from it."
--Malcolm Forbes

"The secret of success is constancy to purpose."
--Benjamin Franklin

"Good is not good where better is expected."
--Thomas Fuller

"The secret of success is sincerity. Once you can fake that you've got it made."
--Jean Giraudoux

"Achievement seems to be connected with action. Successful men and women keep moving. They make mistakes, but they don't quit."
--Conrad Hilton

"You don't become enormously successful without encountering and overcoming a number of extremely challenging problems."
--Mark Victor Hansen

"Time is our most valuable asset, yet we tend to waste it, kill it, and spend it rather than invest it."
--Jim Rohn

"Everyone who got where he is has had to begin where he was."
--Robert Louis Stevenson

How to Be a Network Marketing Millionaire

Remember, you can earn more money, but when time is spent is gone forever.
--Zig Ziglar

"We will either find a way, or make one."
--Hannibal

"I am always doing things I can't do. That's how I get to do them."
--Pablo Picasso

"Never mistake activity for achievement."
--Coach John Wooden

"The harder you fall, the higher you bounce."
--Anonymous

Many marriages would be better if the husband and wife clearly understood that they're on the same side.
--Zig Ziglar

You don't drown by falling in water; you only drown if you stay there.
--Zig Ziglar

"Always bear in mind that your own resolution to succeed is more important than any other one thing."
--Abraham Lincoln

Winner's Blueprint for Achievement

- BELIEVE while others are doubting.
- PLAN while others are playing.
- STUDY while others are sleeping.
- DECIDE while others are delaying.
- PREPARE while others are daydreaming.
- BEGIN while others are procrastinating.
- WORK while others are wishing.
- SAVE while others are wasting.
- LISTEN while others are talking.
- SMILE while others are frowning.
- COMMEND while others are criticizing.
- PERSIST while others are quitting."

--William Arthur Ward

"Everything I've ever done was out of fear of being mediocre."
--Chet Atkins, Guitarist

"A successful person is one who can lay a firm foundation with the bricks that others throw at him or her."
--David Brinkley

"My mother said to me, "If you become a soldier, you'll be a general; if you become a monk, you'll end up as the Pope." Instead, I became a painter and wound up as Picasso."
--Pablo Picasso

"The heights by great men reached and kept
Were not attained by sudden flight,
But they, while their companions slept,
Were toiling upward in the night."
--Henry Wadsworth Longfellow

How to Be a Network Marketing Millionaire

"One ship sails East,
And another West,
By the self-same winds that blow,
Tis the set of the sails
And not the gales,
That tells the way we go."
--Ella Wheeler Wilcox

"Only those who dare to fail greatly can ever achieve greatly."
--Robert F. Kennedy

"Winning is a habit. Unfortunately, so is losing."
--Vince Lombardi

"Success consists of going from failure to failure without loss of enthusiasm."
--Winston Churchill

"There are 12 essential elements to success. The first one is integrity. The other 11 don't matter."
--Ed Mercer, "Mr. Costa Rica"

"You can do anything if you have enthusiasm."
--Henry Ford

"You must do the thing you think you cannot do."
--Eleanor Roosevelt

We are continually faced by great opportunities brilliantly disguised as insoluble problems.

Keep your eyes on the stars and your feet on the ground.
--Theodore Roosevelt

"A pound of pluck is worth a ton of luck."
-- James Garfield, 20th President of the United States

"Talent made a poor appearance. until he married Perseverance."
-- Arthur Guiterman, Editor and Poet

"Outstanding leaders go out of their way to boost the self-esteem of their personnel. If people believe in themselves, it's amazing what they can accomplish."
-- Sam Walton, Founder of Wal-Mart and Sam's Club

"People don't care how much you know. They want to know how much you care."

"Time is more value than money. You can get more money, but you cannot get more time."
-- Jim Rohn, Motivational Speaker

"Trying times get worse when you stop trying."
--Bob Sharpe

"Inaction breeds doubt and fear. Action breeds confidence and courage. If you want to conquer fear, do not sit home and think about it. Go out and get busy."
-- Dale Carnegie, Author

"The greatest manager has a knack for making ballplayers think they are better than they think they are."
-- Reggie Jackson, Baseball Player

"They always say time changes things, but you actually have to change them yourself."
--Andy Warhol

"If you would persuade, you must appeal to interest rather than intellect."
-- Benjamin Franklin

"Poor people have big TVs; Rich people have big libraries"
--Unknown

"The greatest lesson of life is that you are responsible for your life."
-- Oprah Winfrey, talk show host

"The one word that makes a good manager - decisiveness."
-- Lee Iacocca, Auto Executive

"In theory, there is no difference between theory and practice. But in practice, there is."
--Yogi Berra

"Sometimes we stare so long at a door that is closing that we see too late the one that is open."
-- Alexander Graham Bell, Inventor

"I think luck is the sense to recognize an opportunity and the ability to take advantage of it. The man who can smile at his breaks and grab his chances gets on."
-- Samuel Goldwyn, movie executive

"Life isn't about waiting for the storm to pass... ....It's about learning to dance in the rain."
--Unknown

"The door to the room of success swings on the hinges of opposition."
--Dr. Bob Jones

"I don't think of myself as a poor deprived ghetto girl who made good. I think of myself as somebody who from an early age knew I was responsible for myself, and I had to make good."
-- Oprah Winfrey

"Go as far as you can see; when you get there, you'll be able to see farther."
-- J.P. Morgan, industrialist

"Our dreams are defined by our hearts, our future is designed by our dreams"
--Unknown

"Keep your fears to yourself, but share your inspiration with others."
-- Robert Louis Stevenson, writer

"People fail forward to success."
-- Mary Kay Ash

How to Be a Network Marketing Millionaire

"Every strike brings me closer to the next home run."
--Babe Ruth

"An investment in knowledge always pays the best interest."
--Benjamin Franklin

"If you don't design your own life plan, chances are you'll fall
into someone else's plan. And guess what they have planned for
you? Not much."
--Jim Rohn

You Can If You Think You Can!

If you think you are beaten, you are,
If you think you dare not, you don't.
If you like to win, but you think you can't,
It is almost certain you won't.
If you think you'll lose, you're lost,
For out in the world we find,
Success begins with a fellow's will.
It's all in the state of mind.
If you think you are outclassed, you are,
You've got to think high to rise,
You've got to be sure of yourself before
You can ever win a pri.ze.
Life's battles don't always go
To the stronger or faster man.
But soon or late the man who wins,
Is the man who thinks he can."
--C. W. Longenecker

"The discipline of writing something down is the first step toward making it happen."
-- Lee Iacocca

"I am a great believer in luck, and I find that the harder I work, the more I have of it."
---- Thomas Jefferson

"The only thing even in this world are the number of hours in a day. The difference in winning or losing is what you do with those hours."
-- Woody Hayes

"Formal education will make you a living; self-education will make you a fortune."
--Jim Rohn

"Happiness is not a goal; it is a by-product."
-- Eleanor Roosevelt

"Excellence does not come unless failure is an option."
--Dave Ramsey

"If you can find a path with no obstacles, it probably doesn't lead anywhere."
-- Frank A. Clark

"In order for you to profit from your mistakes, you have to get out and make some."
-- Anonymous

How to Be a Network Marketing Millionaire

"An imperfect plan implemented today is better than a perfect plan implemented tomorrow."
--Unknown

"The mind moves in the direction of our currently dominant thoughts."
--Earl Nightingale

"Today I will do what others won't, so tomorrow I can accomplish what others can't."
-- Jerry Rice, NFL Player

"A pessimist sees the difficulty in every opportunity; an optimist sees the opportunity in every difficulty."
-- Winston Churchill

"You'll always miss 100% of the shots you don't take."
-- Wayne Gretzky, Pro Hockey Player

"Faith is taking the first step even when you don't see the staircase."
-- Martin Luther King, Jr.

"I attribute my success to this: I never gave or took an excuse."
-- Florence Nightingale

"Dig the well before you are thirsty."
-- Chinese Proverb

The best time to plant a tree is 20 years ago. The second best time is now.

Age wrinkles the body. Quitting wrinkles the soul.
--Douglas MacArthur

In war there is no substitute for victory.
--Douglas MacArthur

It is fatal to enter any war without the will to win it.
--Douglas MacArthur

There is no security on this earth; there is only opportunity.
--Douglas MacArthur

If fear is cultivated it will become stronger, if faith is cultivated it will achieve mastery.
--John Paul Jones

The best luck of all is the luck you make for yourself.
--Douglas MacArthur

The object of war is not to die for your country but to make the other bastard die for his.
--George S. Patton

Bravery is the capacity to perform properly even when scared half to death.
--Omar N. Bradley

How to Be a Network Marketing Millionaire

A library is not a luxury but one of the necessities of life.
--Rev. Henry Ward Beecher

Children are unpredictable. You never know what inconsistency
they are going to catch you in next.
--Rev. Henry Ward Beecher

Clothes and manners do not make the man; but, when he is made,
they greatly improve his appearance.
--Rev. Henry Ward Beecher

It is not the going out of port, but the coming in, that determines
the success of a voyage.
--Rev. Henry Ward Beecher

It's easier to go down a hill than up it but the view is much better
at the top.
--Rev. Henry Ward Beecher

Our best successes often come after our greatest disappointments.
--Rev. Henry Ward Beecher

You and I do not see things as they are. We see things as we are.
--Rev. Henry Ward Beecher

Life is 10% what happens to you and 90% how you react to it.
--Pastor Charles R. Swindoll

A man must be big enough to admit his mistakes, smart enough to profit from them, and strong enough to correct them.
--John C. Maxwell

The secret of living a life of excellence is merely a matter of thinking thoughts of excellence. Really, it's a matter of programming our minds with the kind of information that will set us free.
--Pastor Charles R. Swindoll

We choose what attitudes we have right now. And it's a continuing choice.
--John C. Maxwell

"Failure is simply the opportunity to begin again - this time more intelligently."
--Henry Ford

"If you aren't fired with enthusiasm, you will be fired with enthusiasm."
-- Vince Lombardi

"Success is a state of mind. If you want success, start thinking of yourself as a success."
-- Joyce Brothers, Psychologist

"When you hate, the only person you hurt is you, because most of the people you hate don't know it, and the other people don't care."
--Medgar Evers, Civil Rights Leader

How to Be a Network Marketing Millionaire

"Bad choices have bad consequences."
--John Mauldin, investment advisor

"I have failed over and over and over. That's why I succeeded."
--Michael Jordan

"A government big enough to give you everything you want is strong enough to take everything you have."
--Thomas Jefferson

"Every artist was first an amateur."
-- Ralph Waldo Emerson

"The problem with socialism is that eventually you run out of other people's money."
--Margaret Thatcher

"There are two primary choices in life: to accept conditions as they exist, or accept the responsibility for changing them."
~ Denis Waitley

"You cain't run from trouble. There ain't no place that far."
--Uncle Remus

"Fret about nothing. Pray about everything. Then you can make it through anything"
--Pastor Fred Lowery, First Baptist Church, Bossier City, LA

"If you find a path without obstacles, it's probably a road that leads nowhere."
--Pastor Fred Lowery, First Baptist Church, Bossier City, LA

"Things are never as good as they seem. Things are never as bad as they seem."
--Pastor Fred Lowery, First Baptist Church, Bossier City, LA

"There is only one way to make a great deal of money, and that is in a business of your own."
-- J. Paul Getty, oil tycoon

"It's better to light a candle than curse the darkness."
-- Eleanor Roosevelt

"Setting a goal is not the main thing. It is deciding how you will go about achieving it and staying with that plan."
-- Tom Landry, football coach

"A pessimist burns his bridges before he gets to them."
 --Unknown

"Hating people is like burning down your own house to get rid of a rat."
--Ralph Waldo Emerson

"The greater danger for most of us lies not in setting our aim too high and falling short, but in setting our aim too low and achieving our mark."
— Michelangelo

How to Be a Network Marketing Millionaire

"The optimist and the pessimist--
The difference is very droll.
The optimist sees the donut;
The pessimist sees the hole."
--John T. Sharpe (my grandfather)

"Each man (is) the architect of his own fortune."
-- Appius Caecus, builder

"Either you run the day or the day runs you."
— Jim Rohn

"Managing is getting paid for home runs someone else hits."
-- Casey Stengel, baseball manager

"I would never have amounted to anything were it not for
adversity. I was forced to come up the hard way."
-- J.C. Penney

"As for worrying about what other people might think - forget it.
They aren't concerned about you. They're too busy worrying
about what you and other people think of them."
-- Michael le Boeuf

"Motivation is what gets you started. Habit is what keeps you
going."
— Jim Ryun: Former track athlete and politician

"Failure is the price of success."
--Bob Sharpe

"People will do anything for those who encourage their dreams, justify their failures, allay their fears, confirm their suspicions and help them throw rocks at their enemies."
--Joe Vitale

"Happiness is not having what you want, but wanting what you have."
--Unknown

"If stupidity got us into this mess, why can't it get us out?"
--Will Rogers

"All saints have a past. All sinners have a future."
--Warren Buffet

"The action you take affects the result you will get."
--Tony Robbins

"Although nobody can go back and make a brand new start, anybody can start from here and make a brand new ending."
--Unknown

"When you get to the end of your rope, tie a knot and hang on."
--Franklin Delano Roosevelt

"Being defeated is often a temporary condition. Giving up is what makes it permanent."
--Marilyn vos Savant

"Success is not final, failure is not fatal; it is the courage to continue that counts."
--Winston Churchill

"We can do anything if we stick to it long enough."
--Helen Keller

"Consider the postage stamp: its usefulness consists in the ability to stick to one thing till it gets there."
--Josh Billings

"Never give up, for that is just the place and time that the tide will turn."
--Harriet Beecher Stowe

"Intellectual growth should begin at birth and cease only at death."
--Albert Einstein

"In network marketing, it's always easier to start in a new company than to succeed in the company you're in. The cost of starting is low. The cost of success is high."
--Bob Sharpe

"Too many people overvalue what they are not and undervalue what they are."
--Malcolm Forbes

"Review your goals twice every day in order to be focused on achieving them."
--Les Brown

"I have always found that if I move with 75% or more of the facts, I usually never regret it. It's the guys who wait to have everything perfect that drive you crazy."
-- Lee Iacocca, executive

"A friend asked a man with a terminal illness how it felt to know that he was going to die. The man replied, 'How does it feel to pretend you are not?'"
--Rich Buhler, KBRT Radio

"Your goals are the road maps that guide you and show you what is possible for your life."
--Les Brown

"If you don't know where you are going, you might wind up someplace else."
--Yogi Berra

"People with goals succeed because they know where they're going."
--Earl Nightingale

"Nothing is more common than unfulfilled potential."
--Professor Howard Hendricks, Dallas Theological Seminary

"The future belongs to those who believe in their dreams."
--Eleanor Roosevelt

"Raise your thoughts and you raise your potential."
--Unknown

"If you want something to change, you have to change something."
--Bob Sharpe

"The man who stops advertising to save money is like the man who stops his clock to save time."
--Thomas Jefferson

"Procrastination is the thief of dreams."
--Wayne Gretzky

"Success in business requires training and discipline and hard work. But if you're not frightened by these things, the opportunities are just as great today as they ever were."
--David Rockefeller

"We confide in our strength without boasting of it; we respect that of others, without fearing it."
-- Thomas Jefferson, 1793

"Patience and perseverance have a magical effect before which difficulties disappear and obstacles vanish."
--John Quincy Adams

"The budget should be balanced, the Treasury should be refilled, public debt should be reduced, the arrogance of officialdom should be tempered and controlled, and the assistance to foreign lands should be curtailed lest Rome become bankrupt. People must again learn to work, instead of living on public assistance."
--Cicero, 55 B.C.

"If you don't think about the future, you won't have one."
--Henry Ford

"If you think you can do it, or you think you can't do it, you are right."
--Henry Ford

"A leader is a dealer in hope."
--Napoleon

"If you do the wrong things, you won't have the right results."
--Tony Cupisz

"One of the penalties of not participating in politics is that you will be governed by your inferiors."
--Plato

"Simplicity is the ultimate sophistication."
--Leonardo da Vanci

"Doers get what they want."
--Jim Kukrai in *Attention! This Book Will Make You Money.*

"The Road to the top is never smooth, but it always leads to the top."
--Bob Sharpe

For God so loved the world that He gave His only begotten Son, that whoever believes in Him should not perish but have everlasting life.

--John 3:16

Network Marketing in College

Network Marketing Curriculum and Center for Servant Leadership Added by Bethany College

www.bethanylb.edu/news-4-11-NetworkMarketingAddedByBethany.html

April 5, 2011

CONTACT Robert Carlson, (785) 227-3380, ext. 8167

NETWORK MARKETING CURRICULUM AND CENTER FOR SERVANT LEADERSHIP ADDED BY BETHANY COLLEGE

LINDSBORG, Kan.— Bethany College will add a new network marketing curriculum in fall 2011. The program was created through Bethany's new Center for Servant Leadership that promotes the awareness, understanding, and practice of servant leadership by individuals and organizations.

Bethany is the first institution to offer network marketing as a major. The program's mission is to promote integrity, trust, and transparency in network marketing. Network marketing is an emerging business model that is under-represented in business education.

Robert Carlson, M.B.A., professor and chair of business, says, "Entrepreneurs have not been taught how to correctly use network marketing. This has led to many using unethical, unsustainable, and nonproductive network marketing business models. We want to fill the education gap and teach students how to use the foundations of servant leadership to successfully and honorably operate a network marketing business."

The curriculum includes both classroom education and experience-based practicum with network marketing mentors. Students will learn business practices, planning requirements, compensation plan variables, product distribution processes, marketing and advertising methods, and industry trends.

Bethany will offer both a major in marketing with emphasis in network marketing and a certificate in network marketing. The major is earned with 56 to 57 credit hours, and the certificate is earned with 15 credit hours.

The Center for Servant Leadership was founded on Robert Greenleaf's characteristics of a servant leader, and its objectives include instilling servant leadership as an interdisciplinary activity, emphasizing responsibility to community, developing leadership skills, and creating sustainable funding sources for program activities. Servant leadership is one of Bethany's five core values.

The Center will act as an umbrella organization to houseservant leadership programs and activities. Carlson will lead these programs as the recently-appointed special assistant to the president for innovation and new ventures. Carlson will help identify and implement projects that meet students' needs and add educational value.

Bethany College, established by Swedish Lutheran immigrants in 1881, is a college of the Evangelical Lutheran Church in America. The mission of Bethany College is to educate, develop and challenge individuals to reach for truth and excellence as they lead lives of faith, learning and service. Bethany College is on the Web at www.bethanylb.edu.

Glossary

48-Hour Rule .... Always follow up within 48 hours whenever possible after your initial contact with a prospect or after a presentation. The fortune is in the follow up. People who don't follow up promptly lose business.

5-Year Plan .... A plan to be financially free in 5 years. It is very possible for a person who follows the instruction and goes to work in a good network marketing company.

Aged Leads .... Leads that are 30-90 days old or more when you purchase them. Aged leads are usually very cheap, because they have been sold 4 or more times before they are sold as aged leads.

Associate .... See *Distributor.*

Autoresponder .... A piece of software or a service that captures the email addresses of interested visitors to your web site and automatically sends a series of follow-up emails to the prospect.

Autoship .... An order for a product that ships and charges your credit card every month. Many nutritional product network marketing companies require a distributor to purchase $50 to $100 worth of products by autoshipment every month in order to get paid.

Back Office .... The private area on the company web site where you can log in and get training information, information about your sales and downline and other things pertinent to your business.

B2B .... *Business-to-Business.* This describes the marketing of products and services to businesses. There are opportunities for professional network marketers to be very profitable in offering business products and services to other businesses.

B2C .... *Business-to-Consumer.* This describes the marketing of products and services to consumers.

Binary .... A network marketing compensation plan where you build your entire business on just 2 legs.

Bizop, or Bizopp .... Short for *Business Opportunity*

Bonus .... Extra money you get for special achievement, over and above your normal pay.

Breakage .... Override or bonus money that goes back to the company because a distributor didn't qualify to get it. While most network marketing companies use breakage to help fund the operations and make profit, some companies do not. See *Compression.*

Business Briefing............A public meeting where a business presentation is made to introduce the business opportunity to new people. Many people join network marketing companies after a presentation at one of these meetings. You can bring your prospects and build your business this way. Also known as an *Opportunity Meeting.*

Cold Market....................The people you don't know whom you are marketing to. You reach your cold market by advertising, networking and talking to people when you are out.

Commission....................The pay you get for making a sale or getting a new customer. Most commissions are paid as a percentage of your gross sales.

Compensation.................The pay you get for doing something.

Compensation Plan..........The schedule of payments a network marketing company pays you for building your business and selling their products. This generally includes all commissions, overrides and bonuses.

Compression...................An element of the compensation plan of some network marketing companies that takes the overrides and bonuses that distributors did not qualify for and awards it to their upline, rather than to the owners of the company. See *Breakage*.

Conference Call ....A phone call where many people can dial in and listen to one or more people speak. In network marketing, conference calls are used for introducing the company to prospects, and for training distributors.

Consultant ....See *Distributor*.

Consumable....................Products or services that are used up regularly and must be purchased over and over, thereby generating repeat income.

Crossline ....A distributor in your network marketing company who is part of another organization, i.e., who is neither in your upline nor downline.

Cycle ....When a specified number of people join your business in a binary or matrix compensation plans, you get paid. When this happens, you are said to *cycle*.

Deduction.......................See *tax deduction*.

Direct Sales ....Selling directly to the end user, either a consumer or another business. Network marketing is one form of direct selling.

Distributor.........................A person who joins a network marketing company to build a business. Some companies use other terms for *distributor*. Some of these terms are *Independent Business Owner (IBO)*, *Independent Representative (IR)*, *Associate, Consultant*, etc.

Domain Name..................The dot-com name of a web site. It is also known as a *URL*.

Downline ....The people who join your business under you. This is your sales team.

Double Opt-In..................The process of requiring a person to ask you twice before adding them to your email list. This protects you from spam complaints and legal problems. Generally, if you are using an *autoresponder* system, a person requests information. A verification email will automatically be sent to them with instructions to click a link to verify they want to be on your list. They will be taken to a screen where they will be instructed to check their email to verify their request. If they don't verify their request, they will not be added to your email list. This is a very common Internet procedure these days.

Exclusive Lead ....A lead that is sold only to you. Most leads you can buy online are sold to 2-4 different network marketers, all from different companies. Exclusive leads are sold only to you, so they are more expensive. Some exclusive leads are resold to other network marketers 60-90 days after they are sold to you.

Federal Trade

Commission .... The federal agency created to protect consumers against unfair methods of competition and deceptive business practices.

Financial Freedom .... The state in which you have enough residual income every month that you can afford your dream lifestyle and you never need to work if you don't want.

Flow, State of .... The state of consciousness where one becomes totally absorbed in what one is doing, to the exclusion of all other thoughts and emotions. This is the technique of marathon runners and network marketers to keep going and finish the race at a time it seems impossible.

Follow Up .... Contacting a person who has expressed interest in being a distributor or a customer.

Forced Matrix.................. A type of compensation plan in which a distributor is required to have a certain number of people on their first 2-3 levels to form a matrix. They then get paid a bonus for filling up the matrix.

Frontloading .... The practice of some companies to try to sell distributors a number of distributorship positions or products that they can resell to new people they recruit. Frontloading is a telltale sign that a company is an illegal pyramid scheme.

FTC .... See *Federal Trade Commission.*

Genealogy .... A report showing everyone who is in your downline and how they are related to you.

Hitting the Wall .... The feeling that it is impossible to go on in your business because there is no way you will be able to succeed. Network marketers who do not know how to handle this experience quit and fail. Network marketers, like marathon runners, must learn how to deal with the wall and operate in the state of *flow* in order to carry on and succeed.

Home Office Deduction .. A tax deduction the IRS allows for people operating a business out of their homes. Consult a tax professional who specializes in home based business tax deductions for information. You can also get more information from the Resources section of www.ITrainMillionaires.com.

Hot Pockets ....Small clear poly envelopes with adhesive on one side. You can put sizzle cards with a toll-free number and a web site to get people's interest in your business opportunity and/or products and services.

IBO.................................Independent Business Owner. See *Distributor.*

Independent
Business Owner ....See *Distributor.*

Independent
Representative.................See *Distributor*

Interactive
Voice Response...............An interactive phone system where you can call and get information about your latest sales and recruits, paychecks and other information about your business over the phone from the company's computer.

IR....................................Independent Representative. See *Distributor*

IVR.................................See *Interactive Voice Response*

Landing Page ....See *Squeeze page.*

Lead...............................Pronounced *leed.* A person who may be interested in becoming a customer or distributor. There are companies that sell network marketing leads. Purchased leads normally range in cost from 5¢ to $5.00 each. Most of the cheap leads are worthless. The best leads are *real time leads.*

Leg................................Each person who is directly under you and all the people under them in your downline. A leg can go any number of levels deep. Some network marketing companies allow you to develop as many legs as you want. Others restrict you to just two legs *(binary systems).*

Level.............................The relative position of your upline and downline business partners to you in your team. The people directly under you are on your first level. They are on your first level whether you personally recruited them, or whether someone in your upline recruited and placed them there. The people on their first level people are on your second level, etc.

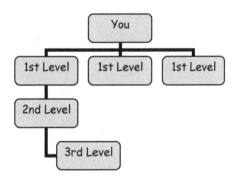

Linear Income.................Income from working a job. You get paid when you work. You don't get paid when you don't work. It is not *residual income.*

Marketing.........................Everything that an individual or a company does to make a sale. Marketing includes advertising, sales, and anything else to put business on the books.

Matrix..............................A type of compensation plan in which a distributor is required to have a certain number of people on their first 2-4 levels to form a matrix. They then get paid a bonus for filling up the matrix.

Mileage Deduction...........The tax deduction the IRS allows for the business miles you put on your car. For many network marketers, this can be a huge deduction. You must document your business miles. Get more information on income tax savings from the Resources section of www.ITrainMillionaires.com.

MLM...............................Multi-level marketing, another name for network marketing.

Multi-Level Marketing.....Another name for network marketing.

Network Marketing..........A type of business where an individual can join a company and earn money from personal sales and from the sales of people he or she recruits, plus the sales of people they recruit on down through a specified number of levels. Most network marketing companies pay on 6-7 levels or more.

Non-Consumable .... Products and services that are typically a one-time purchase, or that or repurchased less than once a year.

Non-Exclusive Leads .... Leads that are sold to 2-4 network marketers when they are generated. When you buy a non-exclusive lead, a few other people are getting it at the same time, so it is important that you try to be the first one to call and make a good impression on the prospect.

Opportunity Meeting .... See *business briefing.*

Opt-In .... The permission you get from another person to send them email about your business. Never start sending advertising emails to people without their permission.

Overhead .... The entire cost of running a business, including rent, payroll, insurance, advertising, marketing, etc. Traditional businesses generally have high overhead. Most network marketing businesses have very low overhead.

Override .... The commissions you earn from the sales of the people in your downline. When you build your business big, 90% or more of your income will come from overrides.

Passive Income.................In network marketing, this is another term for *residual income.* For tax purposes, it is a particular type of residual income.

Payline............................The portion of your downline you get paid overrides on. If your downline has 20 levels and you get paid on the first 7 levels, the people in those first 7 levels constitute your *payline.*

Pay-per-Click..................A form of advertising online where you pay a certain amount every time someone clicks on the link to visit your web site. The sponsored ads at the very top on Google and the ads down the right-hand column are *pay-per-click* ads. These can go for anywhere from a few cents to a few dollars per click, whether your web site visitor stays on the site or clicks away quickly.

PBR................................Private Business Reception.

Phone Surveyed Leads.....The very best leads you can buy if they are also *exclusive leads.* These are people who have been on the phone with the lead company, have confirmed their interest and given information about themselves and what they want. They are expecting a call.

Pin Level ....See *Rank.*

Ponzi Scheme..................An investment swindle in which some early investors are paid off with money put up by later investors in order to encourage more and bigger investments. It is named after Charles Ponzi. Illegal *Pyramid* Schemes are variations of the Ponzi Scheme.

Private
Business Reception.......... A one-on-one presentation.

Product Quadrant............. The way to find the best network marketing products or services to market. Quadrant 1 products are the easiest ones to make money with; Quadrant 4 products are the most difficult.

Prospect .... A person who has expressed interest in your business opportunity, product or service.

Pyramid Scheme.............. A phony network marketing company that pays people for recruiting, and where the money is in the recruiting, not in the sales of legitimate products or services – even if these products or services are legitimate. Pyramid schemes are illegal. If a company charges $500 to join, and it pays you a $200 commission every time you recruit a $500 distributor, it is an illegal pyramid scheme. If your income comes from the products or services your recruit buys, and not the money he pays to join the company, it's legitimate and not a pyramid scheme.

Quadrant 1 Products.........Products or services that customers knew they cannot do without, and that are consumable.

Quadrant 2 Products.........Products or services that customers can do without if they want, and are consumable.

Quadrant 3 Products.........Products or services that customers can do without if they want, but are not consumable.

Quadrant 4 Products.........Products or services that customers can do without if they want, and are not consumable.

Rank ....The level of promotion a distributor has earned in his or her company based on sales and team building. Also known as P*in Level.*

Real Time Leads ....Leads that are transmitted to you within minutes of the time they ask for information online. Many lead companies offer this type of lead. These are normally the best leads you can buy and range in price from $3.00 to $5.00 each.

Recruiting.......................Bringing people into the company to join your sales team.

Residual Income..............Residual Income is the highest form of earned income, because you keep getting get paid over and over for work you did one time. Recording artists get paid for each CD one of their fans buys, even though they only recorded the song once. Network marketers get paid over and over for the recurring sales they make and for the recurring and ongoing sales made by their downline. That is residual income.

Sales Team...................... The people in your downline.

Sizzle Cards.................... Small cards – usually business card size – that get people's attention and direct them to you web site or to call you for more information.

Sizzle Message .... A short audio presentation accessible by phone. Sizzle messages are used to introduce people to your business. After a person listens to the message they are told to contact the person who sent them to the call. Callers cannot leave a message or a callback number.

Sizzle Number .... The phone number used for sizzle calls.

Social Media................... Web sites such as *Facebook* and *Twitter* that allow you to have direct contact with hundreds of people.

Spam.............................. Unsolicited advertising email. Spam causes many problems for legitimate marketers, and it is illegal. If you get spam complaints, your Internet servicing company will cancel your account and you will be without Internet access. In addition, you could be fined or even sued.

Spillover..........................In some compensation plans, you new recruits from your upline may be automatically placed under you. Generally, you will have to recruit a number of people yourself before your spillover will benefit you.

Sponsor (verb).................To recruit a new person into the business.

Sponsor (noun).................The person who recruits a new person into the business. The job of being a good sponsor involves more than recruiting. It involves incubating the new recruit, helping them through the training process, and helping them become profitable in the business.

Squeeze Page ....A one-page web site that has one purpose – to capture the email address and/or phone number of the people who visit the site. A good squeeze page generally lists a lot of benefits and arouses a lot of curiosity and desire to motivate people to provide their contact information and opt-in permission to send them emails.

Stacking..........................The strategy of recruiting people and placing them under a person in your downline. Some companies' compensation plans reward you for stacking; other compensation plans penalize you for it. You need to know the best strategy for placing the people you recruit for your company's compensation plan. Be sure to talk to your upline mentor about the best strategy for your company.

State of Flow................... See *flow, state of*

Tax Deduction .... The amount of money you can legally deduct from your income on tax forms to lower the amount of income you pay income tax on. People who operate home businesses in the US get more legal tax deductions than almost any other class of people, regardless of income level.

Temporary Income .... The income that most people get from working their jobs. They get paid only when they work. For salespeople, most of them only get made when they close a sale and the customer pays. Residual Income, on the other hand, is permanent income, because you keep on getting paid for the work you did.

Three-Way Call .... A phone call in which 3 people in 3 separate locations can participate and talk to one another. These calls are very effective for an upline mentor to use to call prospects with new distributors in training.

Upline.............................Your sponsor and the people above your sponsor in your network marketing company.

Upline Mentor.................Normally your sponsor. If your sponsor is new in the business, a person in your upline who will mentor you as you get started in your business.

URL...............................A web site address. Stands for Uniform Resource Locator. An example of a URL is www.massivepassiveincome.com.

Warm Market..................The people you know, including your friends, relatives, classmates, co-workers, the people you patronize in business, etc. These are the people you should start presenting to when you start your business. As you do, you are learning ways to speak to your cold market.

W4 Form........................In the US, the form you fill out with your employer that is used to calculate the amount of taxes that needs to be deducted from every paycheck to satisfy IRS requirements. When you start a home business, you are allowed more deductions which lower your tax liability. This in turns allows you to rework your W4 form so that you can take home more money from every paycheck.

Webinar .... A "conference call" or seminar on the Internet where participants log in and watch a presentation.

Web Conference .... see *webinar*

Tools and Resources

All the tools and resources mentioned in this
book can be found on our web site.

www.ITrainMillionaires.com

Index

Made in USA - Kendallville, IN
1096725_9780615556543